10 Influen
Entrep

CW01623916

Life-changing Biographies for Teens and Young Adults

Ariana Smith

Copyright © 2023 Ariana Smith. All rights reserved.

The contents of this book may not be reproduced, duplicated, or transmitted without direct written permission from the author.

Under no circumstances will any legal responsibility or blame be held against the publisher for any reparation, damages, or monetary loss due to the information herein, either directly or indirectly.

Legal Notice:

This book is copyright protected. This is only for personal use. You can't amend, distribute, sell, use, quote, or paraphrase any part of the content within this book without the consent of the author.

Disclaimer Notice:

Please note the information contained within this document is for educational and entertainment purposes only. Every attempt has been made to provide accurate, up to date, and reliable complete information. No warranties of any kind are expressed or implied. Readers acknowledge that the author is not engaging in the rendering of legal, financial, medical, or professional advice. The content of this book has been derived from various sources.

By reading this document, the reader agrees that under no circumstances is the author responsible for any losses, direct or indirect, which are incurred as a result of the use of information contained within this document, including, but not limited to, errors, omissions, or inaccuracies.

ISBN 978-9916-9870-8-7 (eBook)
ISBN 978-9916-9870-7-0 (paperback)
ISBN 978-9916-9870-6-3 (hardcover)

www.ariana-smith.com

Contents

Something for You!

Get your printable business plan template today!

One of the biggest challenges you'll ever face is to accept there is no limit to what you can do. This free business plan template will help you think through the key elements of your own business!

Scan this code to download.

Introduction

Have you ever found yourself needing a tool or product that does not exist? This is how entrepreneurs are born—they understand the *need* for that one thing which does not yet exist, and they then aim to produce and supply it to others who may need it, too.

But it's not all that easy at first. In order to make a product that does not yet exist, the person making it will need money to have it produced, and also to promote and market the product. In most cases, they will turn to people who have money to invest in a new business. But they will need to provide the investor with a solid business plan and promise of success if they expect the investor to give them any money at all.

No, not everyone gets it right the first time. But a good entrepreneur also knows that first-time failure is not a reason to give up. Instead of quitting, they look more closely at what it was that did not work the first time around, and they fix it. A good entrepreneur, therefore, learns from failure, and uses it as an opportunity to perfect either the product or the plan they've designed to see it reach the right market.

Challenges and failures are, indeed, part of our life. Think of a toddler learning to walk; we all fell over the first time, but we tried and tried again until we got it right. With each attempt at trying to do something we've not done before, we gain valuable experience that makes us wiser and better equipped to reach our desired goal.

Nobody is perfect, which is why we should not compare ourselves with others. Each of us has a unique gift, our own unique signature and character which others do not have, and so it is only for ourselves that we should continue to try to do better, until we hit our own desired target. There is no need to judge ourselves harshly, as long as we are always putting our best into what we do.

With support and understanding from family and friends, there is never any need to quit on our ambitions. When we love and believe in ourselves and our dreams, we in turn serve as role models to others who want to fulfill their goals, too. As long as we do not bring harm to others or the environment in our quest for success, we will be supported.

This book has been written for you and others like you; young women who might be unsure about their life path but have ideas they would like to share with the world, in hopes their idea will fulfill a need, or even a want. The women whose biographies we cover here also began with nothing to very little, much as you might be.

Their stories are inspiring and will help you to see that all challenges and obstacles can be overcome when you have sincere passion and love for your dreams and goals. These role models serve as guides to steer you in the right direction, to help you become the best 'you' you can be, so you will reach full success as an entrepreneur.

My name is Ariana Smith. I am an author, a mother, a wife, and also a successful entrepreneur, sharing knowledge with you, the younger generation, in hopes it will help you discover your true potential, feel empowered, and continue into the future with high moral standards.

"Success is not the key to happiness. Happiness is the key to success. If you love what you are doing, you will be successful."

- Albert Schweitzer

Eliza Lucas

1722 - 1793

"A variety of employment gives my thoughts a relief from melancholy subjects." - Eliza Lucas

Who Was Eliza?

Elizabeth Lucas Pinckney, fondly known as Eliza, was born on the Caribbean Island of Antigua in the West Indies (a colony of Great Britain) on December 28th, 1722. She is known for her efforts towards agriculture in colonial South Carolina, where she discovered that the Indigo plant (Indigofera tinctoria) could be used as the perfect dye for clothing. Focusing on becoming the most successful Indigo production farm in the region, she achieved her goal, and her crops went on to produce one-third of the colony's export value. She herself managed three of the plantations.

Elizabeth grew up on a plantation farm known as 'Poorest,' a sugarcane plantation belonging to her family. She was the eldest child in her family, which consisted of her mother, Ann, and her father, Colonel George Lucas, as well as two brothers and one sister.

As a young girl she was sent to London to receive her education, even though at the time, many women believed that learning to become a mother and housewife was more important than being accomplished. It was not long before she discovered her love for botany, and soon, her skills were recognized.

At sixteen, in 1738, her father decided his family would be safer in South Carolina, considering the disputes going on between Spain and England around the West Indies at the time. In South Carolina, they began to work on the three plantations they had inherited from Eliza's grandfather, John Lucas: Garden Hill, Waccamaw River, and Wappoo Creek. The family chose to live at Wappoo.

In 1739, her father (whom Eliza held close to her heart) had to return to Antigua to address the unrest between England and Spain. Sadly, it was not long after this that her mother passed away. Eliza was left to run the plantations on her own.

Still only sixteen-years-old, she managed the Wappoo plantation alone, while also supervising the overseers on both of the other plantations; the first produced tar and timber, while the second produced rice. She would write daily about the decisions she made for all of them, with her 'letter-books' now being in the hands of the South Carolina Historical Society. During her initial years at the Wappoo plantation, Eliza also took care of her younger sister, Mary, while her brothers continued to study in London.

Her father continued to send her seeds for trials on the plantations, some of which supplemented their cultivation of rice. Mostly, Elizabeth experimented with ginger, cotton, alfalfa, and hemp, but on realizing the demand for dye made from the indigo plant, she persevered through failed attempts, until she proved it could be successfully grown on South Carolina soil. She accepted assistance from an indigo-maker of African descent, whom her father had hired from the French West Indies. . .

In 1744, she shared her seeds with other planters, which ultimately led to dramatically increased indigo exports from South Carolina. Because of Eliza, indigo became the South Carolina colony's commodity cash crop. It was also in 1744 that Eliza married Charles Pinckney, her lifelong friend, with whom she went on to have four children: three sons (one of whom died during infancy) and one daughter.

Charles, too, owned a few plantations. Had Eliza not possessed the autonomy and economic power she did, she would not have been able to marry Charles and would have had to marry one of the suitors her father had recommended.

In 1753, the family moved to London, where they stayed for five years. Sadly, in 1758, Charles passed away due to malaria, and Eliza ran both her and his plantations on her own, using her profits to further her children's 'progressive' education, which ultimately saw her sons being able to play major roles in the American Revolution.

It is important to note that Charles was also an influential colonizer, as well as a signatory of the United States Constitution. During the Revolutionary Wars, however, Charles' plantations were destroyed by British troops.

In 1793, struggling with breast cancer and trying to find a cure for it, Eliza went to a hospital in Philadelphia for treatment. Despite efforts by doctors, she passed away on May 27th. Elizabeth was deeply respected, and she was honored at her funeral through President George Washington's choice to be a pallbearer.

In 1989, Elizabeth became the first woman to be inducted into the South Carolina Hall of Fame, with a tribute given in appreciation of her initiative and great efforts and contributions towards creating South Carolina's thriving agricultural sector.

Eliza's Motivation

Eliza loved school and highly valued her education at boarding school in England, where she studied music and French, with her favorite subject being botany. Whenever she wrote to her father, she would always emphasize that education was a more valuable fortune than anything else he could have given her, and that it would certainly make her happy in her future life. Through this, Eliza demonstrated a passion for learning, and where there is passion, there is always motivation.

Eliza was always curious about new methods of learning, too, which is what allowed her to tolerate all failures when it came to the growing of her crops. She knew that success can be achieved through the elimination of error, and through producing a product more valuable than others already available

With her own children, she also experimented with early-childhood education, following the theories of John Locke, an English philosopher and physician who believed that the human mind is a 'blank slate' at birth, with all personal experiences creating impressions. This way of thinking allowed her to be open-minded and willing to try new things, never afraid of failure.

Her initial determination stemmed from not wanting her family's crops to fail. As they had incurred some debt, she worked to find solutions that would yield good cash-crops and, ultimately, pull her family out of their poor financial situation. Once she had discovered the indigo plant and the demand for it as a dye used to color textiles, especially in England, she set her course for success, and never looked back.

More about her tenacious and experimental personality can be seen through her writings, which consist of a number of volumes centered around her daily life at home and on the plantations. It is said that her writings '*provide a valuable glimpse into the life of an elite colonial woman living during this time period*'[1]. These 'letter-books' were subsequently published in 1850 as 'The Journal and Letters of Eliza Lucas.'

And so, we can see that Elizabeth's motivation was born of the desire, at first, to want to help her family out of their financial struggles. But, of course, this was not the sole reason for her motivation. She had, indeed, grown up the same way—always wanting to know more, always wanting to break matters down into their constituent parts or tasks, so she could more clearly examine the issues standing in the way of success, or even discover the initially unseen clues that, if followed, could lead to greater success.

Perhaps you have a similar mind to Elizabeth, in that you can see a gap in the market and already have an idea for a way to fill it with something you can produce. If you feel as motivated and determined as she did, you are already halfway to becoming a successful entrepreneur.

How Eliza Changed the World for Women

Elizabeth was family-orientated and focused on solutions that would bring prosperity to the greater whole rather than just to herself.

Being family-orientated, she became a strong symbol for wives and mothers also doing their best to raise a family while running a business at the same time. She showed the world that 'breaking the glass ceiling' does not always require a woman to abandon her home and family, that family comes first, and when we attempt to reach success in the name of our families, the results can be as great as the results achieved by women who choose to live a life where they separate their career-life from their home-life.

In simple terms, she was an excellent 'work from home' Mom, who placed as much importance on raising her children and family as she did on her work. She firmly believed that educating a family effectively amounts to producing children who will grow to be successful adults, and also clever in money matters and innovation.

Eliza's tenacity can also be seen in her continuing to run the family plantations for thirty years after her husband's death—this certainly amplifies the elements of dedication and commitment she possessed. Eliza never had an affair, either, and remained true to herself, her husband, and children.

She also proved that sharing knowledge leads to great results for all; that the simple act of sharing, even just a little, can make an entire State great again. Without a doubt, her willingness to learn from others played a big role in her success. She was a real woman in a man's world, not a woman trying to be a man. She embodied the essence of the feminine through careful nurturing and an open, solution-seeking mind.

Eliza's Legacy

Perhaps the most important legacy Eliza left behind is embodied in her efforts to bring prosperity to her community and the State of South Carolina. Her actions could never be seen as simply self-fulfilling because she shared what knowledge and expertise she had, in hopes of bringing fortune and success to all of the people.

She was educated, independent, and accomplished, and began developing these traits at a very early age. She was also dedicated and loyal, which can be seen through her only ever having had one husband and choosing to remain unmarried even years after his passing. Such loyalty and focus are worthy of respect, and were a winning factor with regard to the trust other business partners invested in her.

In 1753, while in London, Eliza gave a silk dress to the Dowager Princess of Wales which had been made from the silk produced on the Pinckney Plantations. This was a gift that would be treasured for years to come and helped to establish relations in trade and production between South Carolina and England.

As previously mentioned, in 1793, upon her passing, President George Washington served as a pallbearer at her funeral, helping to carry Elizabeth's coffin—a gesture seen as both an honor and a sincere gesture of respect.

In 1989, long after her death, Eliza was recognized for her major contributions to South Carolina's thriving agricultural sector, by being the first woman to be added to the South Carolina Business Hall of Fame. This, too, was a great honor and well represents the legacy she left behind.

Beyond her achievements as an entrepreneur, pioneer, and businesswoman, she was also respected for the ways in which she took care of her family. Indeed, Eliza took her family responsibilities seriously, which can be seen through a vow she made about the matter:

"*To make a good wife to my dear husband in all its several branches; to make all my actions correspond with that sincere love and duty I bear him . . . I am resolved to be a good mother to my children, to pray for them, to set them good examples, to give them good advice, to be careful both of their souls and bodies, to watch over their tender minds.*"[2]

What Can We Learn from Eliza's Story?

Perhaps the most important takeaway from Eliza's life story is that she never gave up on her goals. One can only imagine how many failures she faced on the plantations, and how many obstacles lay in her way at the start.

Thriving on the love of family and her intention to bring prosperity to her community and to Carolina, Eliza never let go of the independent streak she'd developed at a very early age. She knew that nothing new can ever be handed to anyone on a silver plate, that if she wanted to achieve her goals, she would have to do everything within her own power to ensure success. Her determination and tenacity were apparent in both her career and her personal life, which meant she had integrity and authenticity, and, in this way, she gained the trust of many very important people and officials.

It is known that some of the best companies of our time function as well as they do due to the team spirit or 'family-vibe' apparent within that company. When those at the top treat their workers like family, with respect and care, a company will function at its best.

And so, through observing the life, traits, and achievements of Elizabeth Lucas, we learn the importance of treating others with respect, as together, much like a family, all involved strive for the highest. And when we do this, we all benefit—not just one person. Eliza teaches us to learn from mistakes, constantly find new solutions to problems, and to put family first.

Lydia Pinkham

1819 - 1883

> ***"Only a woman can understand a woman's ills."***
> – Lydia Pinkham

Who Was Lydia?

Lydia Estes Pinkham, also known as 'Lily the Pink,' was born in the manufacturing city of Lynn, Massachusetts, on February 9th, 1819. She was the tenth-born in a family of twelve children. As a herbalist who went on to become an inventor and marketer of her own products, she created a herbal-alcoholic 'Women's Tonic' that served to heal symptoms which come with menstrual and menopausal issues in women. While at the start her remedy was seen as 'quack' (a hoax), it became so popular, it is still sold around the world today.

Isaac Pinkham, a shoe manufacturer, was twenty-nine-years-old when he and Lydia married, in 1843. Lydia, at that time, chose to devote her life to perfecting her remedy for women's ailments, while raising her family of four children for thirty years, after having worked as a school teacher since 1835. Her remedies were made from a vegetable compound, and it was said it could cure any female complaint, from nervous prostration to a prolapsed uterus.

In 1873, with her family being left in financial turmoil because Isaac had failed to pay back his debts and was sued as a result, she began to share her remedies with local neighbors. By 1875, her remedy was being sold for just $1 a bottle, and it was trusted by many. She marketed her own products through handwritten flyers and pamphlets that read, "Only a woman can understand a woman's ills."

After gathering a little profit, her son decided it would be a good idea to advertise her tonic in the newspaper, and that featuring a photograph of her face would lead to the market trusting the product more. Through using her photograph in the ads, it was not long before she was referred to as 'the savior of her sex'. Then, in 1876, she finally patented her formula.

Lydia would offer her time and knowledge via the written word, by allowing women to send her letters with information about their symptoms and ailments. She would then respond to them, suggesting her remedy. This was a cost-effective way to market her own product, and it worked. She then went on to write a 'facts-of-life' manual for women, and she distributed it for free under various titles.

However, due to her product never having been tested by medical professionals, namely the FDA, in the 1920s, the Lydia E. Pinkham Medicine Co. had to reduce its claims in order to meet the federal regulations of 'drugs in advertising'. But due to her customers' many positive opinions and testimonials, which included statements of satisfaction from a few influential leaders, her product continued to be sold.

Lydia's products soon grew in popularity, even though many institutions tried to discredit her remedies as working only due to the 'placebo effect,' where if you believe the 'cure' is working, it will work. However, plants most certainly do contain healing properties, and it could not be denied that much of the healing came from the herbs she used.

With the increased popularity of her brand, two of her sons, Will and Dan, expanded the reach of her advertising and products, from as far as New York to New England, and, eventually, her herbal women's formula was in demand across the country.

Sadly, despite her being an inventor of the herbal tonic she sold, neither of her sons were able to withstand the side effects of tuberculosis. Both died in 1881. Lydia struggled to come to terms with their passing, and she turned to spiritualism in an attempt to 'speak' to them in the afterlife. However, just one year later, she suffered a paralytic stroke, which led to her passing a year afterwards, at age 64, on May 17th, 1883.

Her son Charles continued to run her successful business, which now featured a number of laboratories and, of course, support from users. At the time of her death, the value of sales of her products was estimated at $300.000 per year. By the 1890s, her compound was the most advertised patent medicine in the USA.

In 1968, the family company was sold, and the production of Lydia's remedies began in Puerto Rico.

In 1922, Lydia's daughter Aroline, who had grown up with the family business, went on to open the Lydia E. Pinkham Memorial Clinic in Salem, Massachusetts, with the intention of providing effective health services to both young mothers as well as their children.

By 1925, long after her passing, sales of Lydia's vegetable compound rose to an astronomical $3 million per year.

More recently, in 1987, Numark Laboratories secured a license to produce Lydia's medicine, choosing to name it 'Lydia Pinkham's Vegetable Compound', which is still found today in various forms, including the 'Lydia Pinkham Herbal Tablet Supplement' and the 'Lydia Pinkham Herbal Liquid Supplement.'

Not only did Lydia create an effective herbal compound to help women, but she also brought to the surface, through advertising, the need for remedies in the area of women's health. She made it clear that women are equal to men with regards to rights, and that they have specific needs due to their physiology.

Once it was realized just how effective using a photograph of a living person (the inventor and producer of the products herself) was, many other advertisers followed suit.

And so, it can be said that besides inventing and marketing a good product for women, she also paved the way for advertisers with regards to the effectiveness of using real people and photographs in advertising to best move a product.

Lydia's Motivation

Perhaps the main motivator behind Lydia's success was a financial one. Having hit rock bottom due to her husband's inability to pay back his debts, their family was left in crisis.

She knew her herbal tonic was good; even if it did not cure any of the ailments it addressed, it surely did soothe them. For this fact alone, it became extremely popular and somewhat essential to many women.

One can say that she made the formula for herself at the start, sharing it with friends, in hopes it would bring them some relief, but she had no idea that, with a bit of marketing and promotion, she would be able to reach a huge audience, and in turn profit from her remedy.

Starting out very small, from her own home, she was able to eventually acquire a larger building or laboratory, where she was able to manufacture her remedy on a large scale. Fortunately, she had two sons who were also motivated—and clearly great thinkers, too—they were responsible for convincing her to feature a photographic image of her head, neck, and shoulders on the product itself and in advertising materials.

Would she have considered this on her own, one might ask? However, her sons were family, and they took over her business after her passing, and so, it can be said she was fortunate to have 'new thinkers' as sons, who ultimately helped her and the family overall, to make the tonic as famous as it still is today.

Financial collapse is often one of the best motivators for those starting a new business. Fortunately, Lydia already had an existing product to market and sell. And the faith bestowed in her product by those who used it certainly increased the product's popularity.

How Lydia Changed the World for Women

The toughest challenge Lydia had to face was the doubt from those in the medical industry. Just as her product became popular, there were attempts to shut her down. If this had happened, she and her family would have been left destitute.

In fact, experts in the medical field went as far as to claim her tonic was a "*valueless preparation kept on the market for about fifty years by means of lying advertisements and worthless testimonials.*"[3]

And so, through Lydia's story, we can see how she played an important role in the lives of women through simply remaining determined and believing in her product, enough to feel totally confident when presenting it to other women—who were often her peers.

Beyond this, though, she was also a strong activist when it came to fighting against slavery, and also for women's rights, as well as an important member of a number of reform groups for abolition, Swedenborgianism, phrenology, and temperance, among other causes. Lydia entered the Lynn Female Anti-Slavery Society at the age of sixteen-years-old, and strongly supported the feminist and moral views of abolitionist author Nathaniel P. Rogers.

Although it is agreed that Lydia's initial motivation for the distribution and marketing of her tonic was fear of financial collapse, many modern-day feminists continue to admire her for making available important information about menstruation and the facts of life.

Many of them consider her to be a 'crusader' for women's health issues as well, considering most medical establishments at the time paid no attention to the issues faced only by women, which resulted in poor service. Due to her successes in this field, the Lydia Pinkham House, nearby her production factory at Western Ave in Lynn, Massachusetts, was added to the National Register of Historic Places on September 25th, 2012.

Lydia's Legacy

Lydia gained much support from women in need during her time, and her legacy certainly still lives on today.

Her herbal tonic not only helped people, but it also became the subject of controversy as well over time, with some medical professionals saying it was not a cure for any ailment, or that it was simply the alcohol content in the formula that made people feel better.

There are even songs, movies, and writings that refer to either her or her formula, which some say her husband, Isaac, was given in place of money to pay back a debt. This was not proven, however, and Lydia denied such accusations.

Some films which make reference to her tonic include:

1. *The Cameraman* from 1928; when the lead character shows a photo of a woman to the doorman, the doorman says, "Maybe it's Lydia Pinkham."

2. *The Penguin Pool Murder* from 1932 sees a crime sleuth teasing his secretary, who wears too much make-up, by saying, "Okay, Lydia Pinkham."

3. *Footlight Parade* from 1933 sees the lead actress saying, "And I'm Lydia Pinkham!"

4. In an episode of *Columbo* ("Lovely but Lethal") from 1973, the lieutenant says to the owner of a cosmetic company, "You're like Lydia Pinkham."

5. *The Handmaid's Tale* from 1985 has the lead female actress named after Lydia Pinkham's Vegetable Compound.

It is true that Lydia's picture was the first used in advertising, in a time where just about all advertising featured men only. Her face went viral—or as viral as it could in a time without mass media—in the Victorian media.

Even college boys would sing about her, namely, a song that actually became popular titled 'Lily the Pink,' later popularized in different versions recorded by the bands 'The Irish Rovers' and 'The Scaffold'.

Beyond this, many women who have seen her as a pioneer in women's health have written books, articles, and made documentaries about Lydia. Through depictions like these, we can see that she surely has left her mark.

While some would say Lydia's remedies were useless and offered no real cure, some women trusted them so much, they would travel to Lynn just to purchase their 'medicines' from her. It is also said that in a time when male doctors were the only physicians available, women preferred to turn to Lydia for advice and help. This, of course, also makes Lydia a cornerstone in the introduction of women practitioners in the medical field. It was Lydia's biographer, Sarah Stage, who wrote, '*In the absence of readily available, valid medical therapies, the Vegetable Compound made sense.*'[4]

All of the efforts Lydia put into her company and producing her tonics pointed towards the depiction of 'the Perfect Wife', meaning one that was not so ill as to be a burden to her husband. Indeed, according to Professor of Sociology at Cornell College Tori Barnes-Brus, Lydia's company became somewhat of a '*social authority on women's reproduction*'[5], and for this she will always be remembered.

What Can We Learn from Lydia's Story?

Perhaps the main message we can take from Lydia's life is one of resilience. Not many people are able to take the criticism and doubt that was so often placed on her. She had to truly believe in her product, which she did, in order for others to believe in it, too.

She showed others that all it takes to make it in the business world is a unique product which is ultimately helpful to others. She also teaches us that accepting help from others is very important when starting a new business. Not everyone gets a helping hand, but she had her family, her sons and a daughter, to help her create a business model and suggest ideas for advertising, as well as assist her in setting up factories and seeing to the distribution of her formulas.

A family built on such mutual trust is powerful, and with the help of her family, Lydia was able to not only pull them out of poverty, but also to accelerate them into a very fruitful future that saw her children content, self-sufficient, and secure in their grown-up lives, as well.

Persevering is the word that perhaps best describes Lydia's nature. Again, even in the face of doubt, she trusted in her family, her product, and herself, leading her to become one of the most recognized and respected women entrepreneurs and businesswomen of the century.

Madam C.J. Walker (Sarah Breedlove)

1876 - 1919

> ***"I got my start by giving myself a start."***
> – Sarah Breedlove

Who Was Sarah?

Born as Sarah Breedlove on December 23rd, 1876, in Delta, Fifth Military District (Louisiana), in the USA, Madam C.J. Walker was the first in her family of five siblings to be born to freedom, after Abraham Lincoln signed the Emancipation Proclamation.

Orphaned at the age of seven, at age ten, Sarah moved to Vicksburg, Mississippi, where she lived with her brother and worked as a domestic servant. She did not receive a formal education and stated that her only education was through lessons at Sunday School.

Living with her brother was not easy as he was an abuser, and this ultimately led to her being married at age fourteen, to Moses McWilliams. Together, they had one daughter, A'Lelia. Unfortunately, Moses passed when Sarah was twenty, in 1887, leaving her to raise two-year-old A'Lelia alone.

In 1888, she moved to St. Louis, where she worked as a laundress, earning less than two dollars per day. She persevered, however, as she deeply wanted her daughter to receive a formal education. The community within which she lived was one that saw the development of Ragtime Music. Singing with the Paul African Methodist Episcopal

Church, she would watch the other more privileged women and yearned to live an educated life as they did.

During this time, she developed bad skin problems, especially scalp-related, due to her poor living conditions. However, her other brothers working in St. Louis were barbers, and they taught her about hair care.

She remarried in 1894, but then divorced her second husband, John Davis, in 1903. It was in 1904 that Sarah gained employment selling hair-care products for Annie Malone, an African American hair-care entrepreneur and millionaire. Shortly after this, in 1905, Sarah moved to Denver, Colorado, where she put her thinking cap on and created her own hair-care product line. While she continued to work for Annie Malone, she progressed in the development of her own hair-care business, as well.

In 1906, she married again, to Charles Joseph Walker, which saw her adopt the name Madam C.J. Walker. However, by this time she had learned to market herself as an independent hairdresser and seller of cosmetic creams, walking door-to-door to teach other black women how to treat their hair.

The business became successful, and soon, she was working via mail order, with A'Lelia (her daughter) in charge, and Charles traveling much of the States to promote and expand the business. In 1908, they moved to Pittsburgh, Pennsylvania, where they opened a beauty parlor, as well as the 'Lelia College,' where they trained other women to become 'hair culturists.' Sarah then offered training programs in the form of 'the Walker System' for her licensed sales agents, who earned through commission.

Sarah then went on to open offices in Indianapolis and New York, as well, and in 1910, she established the headquarters for the Madam C.J. Walker Manufacturing Company, purchasing a house and factory to set up her beauty school, as well as a laboratory to do further research in the field. Between 1911 and 1919, Madam C.J. had several thousand employees working for her company. She also added value to her staff training by teaching her employees how to budget and build their own businesses.

In 1912, Madam C.J. divorced Charles, but continued to succeed at her business. In 1917, the National Beauty Culturists and Benevolent Association of Madam C. J. Walker Agents was established, and this marked the true success she had achieved through her efforts.

Sadly, Sarah developed kidney ailments and hypertension by the age of fifty-one-years-old. She passed on May 25th, 1919, and was buried at Woodland Cemetery in the Bronx, New York.

She was the wealthiest African American woman at the time of her passing. An obituary was written for her in the *New York Times*, where it was stated: '*She'd hoped to be a millionaire, not for herself, but for the good she could do with the money.*'[6]

Sarah's Motivation

Sarah often claimed, "*I had little or no opportunity when I started out in life, having been left an orphan, and being without mother or father since I was seven years of age.*"[7]

At an annual gathering for the National Negro Business League, she stated, "*I am a woman who came from the cotton fields of the South. From there, I was promoted to the washtub. From there, I was promoted to the cook kitchen. And from there, I promoted myself into the business of manufacturing hair goods and preparations. I have built my own factory on my own ground.*"[8]

Without a doubt, Sarah's story is one which many successful women identify with—they too grew up in a life filled with struggle, but they were not prepared to stay down. Sarah strived to fill a gap in the hair-care market, and although she started out with small steps, she maintained her pace without thwarting others—with blinkers on, she moved from strength to strength, achieving all she set out to along the way.

She was obviously a kind person at heart, as well; otherwise, people would not initially have even allowed her into their homes. Her products became a necessity to many women, and this is the core principle that lies at the center of any successful entrepreneurial venture—provide something that is truly needed, and success will follow.

Although she focused on her own business, she did not live for herself only. She greatly supported and also funded the YMCA in the Indianapolis black community, and also contributed scholarship funds to the Tuskegee Institute, Flanner House, the Bethel African Methodist Episcopal Church, the Mary McLeod Bethune's Daytona Education and Industrial Centre for Negro Girls, the Palmer Memorial Institute, and the Haines Normal and Industrial Institute. This led to her being seen as not only an entrepreneur, but also a philanthropist, giving back to society in ways she saw fit.

As her popularity grew, she also began to involve herself in political issues, hoping to bring change in this area, too—which she did. During the First World War, Sarah was a leader in the Circle for Negro War Relief and advocated for the development of a training camp for black army officers. In 1917, she sat on the executive committee of the National Association of Colored People (NACP), which honored her for making the largest individual contribution to help preserve Fredrick Douglas' Anacostia House, as well as their anti-lynching fund. The NACP committee organized the "Silent Parade" that took place in New York in July 1917, with more than ten-thousand people marching to protest about the East Saint riots, which had resulted in the deaths of thirty-nine African Americans.

When she passed, she left nearly one-hundred-thousand dollars to various orphanages, institutions, and individuals, again showing that her motivation throughout her life was certainly to assist others in becoming more than their circumstances would have usually allowed.

Sarah teaches us that wealth comes through giving back to society and our communities; that in order to become respected and heard in any society, we have to work for it and remain focused on our goals, keeping the bigger picture at the forefront, always knowing that acts of selflessness render a greater reward to the whole, and that having such purpose is the real reason for our existence.

How Sarah Changed the World for Women

Sarah Breedlove was patient, humble, and focused. With these attributes, she carried herself to new heights in the business world. Understanding life and its challenges, she took the ups with the downs and remained dedicated to her goals. She had no ego and did what she did to help others, through providing jobs and income through teaching them how the business world works, and offering motivation that saw her trainees follow a somewhat 'Tortoise and Hare' path, where remaining focused and determined is the best way to win.

Her persona was respectful as she sought to overcome discrimination, and she understood that success is limitless when one remains true to one's purpose and aspirations. She was a great representative for women in industry and maintained a calm demeanor that meant she was always heard and acknowledged, never causing trouble, nor seeking attention in order to oust her competition.

She flowed in this way, taking one step at a time, persevering through challenges calmly, without turning tables or making fires that could have landed her in trouble. Sarah had empathy for others, and she understood that the struggles she had been through in her early years were lessons which would ultimately shape her into being one of the world's most successful entrepreneurs and businesswomen, without question or discredit.

Passive in nature, she was somewhat of a Mama Bear, ensuring her cubs were safe and self-sufficient, prepared for life's knocks, and equipped with tools and skills to see them through adversity and help them reach success.

One might say it was not so much her products that led to her success as much her calm and respectful demeanor. Tenacious is a great word to describe her personality, and through such tenacity, she left no stone unturned, always seeking the simplest, truest, and most viable routes to achievement.

Sarah's Legacy

Madame C.J. Walker was known for being a giver, a philanthropist who did her best to help those who would then, in turn, help society. As an activist she accomplished a great deal. Her personal papers have been preserved with the Indiana Historical Society, and two of her properties are listed in the National Register of Historic Places, namely Villa Lewaro in Irvington, New York, which was sold to the Companions of the Forest Organization in 1932, and the

Madame Walker Theater Center in Indianapolis, which included the company's offices, the factory, beauty school, hair salon, barbershop, restaurant, drugstore, and a ballroom for the community.

She also had a museum in Atlanta named in her honor, as well as a historic radio station known as WERD. In 2006, Regina Taylor wrote a play called *The Dreams of Sarah Breedlove* featuring Sarah's struggles and successes.

In 1987, Stanley Nelson created a documentary called *Two Dollars and a Dream*, covering Sarah's life from when she first began working at two dollars an hour to the time she built her own haircare empire. In 1993, she was added to the National Women's Hall of Fame in Seneca Falls, and in 1998, the U.S. Postal Service issued a Madam Walker Commemorative Stamp as part of its Black Heritage series. Then, in 2020, actress Octavia Spencer portrayed Sarah in a TV series called *Self Made*, which is inspired by the Life of Madam C.J. Walker.

To show how her legacy continues to this day, in January of 2022, Sundial Brands, a division of Unilever, launched a collection of eleven products under the brand name 'MADAM' by Madam C.J. Walker.

Many awards have also been named after Sarah, including the Madam C. J. Walker Business and Community Recognition Awards, Spirit Awards—The Madame C.J. Walker Heritage Award.

It is recognition like this that proves the impact she left on society, and for her tenacity and innovations, she will always be remembered.

What Can We Learn from Sarah's Story?

Perhaps the most important lesson we can learn from Sarah Breedlove's story is respect. During a time when many women were choosing to 'break the glass ceiling' through rising up and demanding equal rights and privileges, she kept only her goal in mind, using logic and reason to determine which steps to take, and which paths to avoid.

With a calculating mind, she knew that speaking at one volume and being consistent in her business, without inviting threat or risk, would ensure she was heard and understood.

Many teenage girls these days can feel intimidated by others more successful than themselves. Sarah did not feel that way, and she was able to override peer pressure and any doubts she might have had by staying close to her truth and dedicating her time and emotions towards seeing her own plan unfold.

She teaches us that success comes through showing respect and offering sound, irrefutable plans of action which, when implemented with patience, can lead to new levels of achievement. Sarah also teaches us that there are no limits to how people can help one another: that just because you have achieved one goal does not mean you should stop there—that with each achievement comes the opportunity to create and then reach another goal.

Coco Chanel

1883 – 1971

"The most courageous act is still to think for yourself. Aloud." – Coco Chanel

Who Was Coco?

Coco Chanel, born Gabrielle Bonheur Chanel, is listed by *Time Magazine* as being one of the top one hundred most influential people of the twentieth century. Throughout her adult life she never saw a dull moment, from fashion designer to perfume creator, wartime spy to filmmaker, muse to art collector, she moved in circles that would leave others dizzy.

Born on August 19th, 1883, in Saumur, France, her childhood was less than comfortable and filled with strife. With six siblings, she lived in a one-roomed apartment until age eleven when her mother passed away, after which her father sent her to the convent of Aubazine, an orphanage, where she learned to sew. For six years, she lived at the orphanage, and then was employed as a seamstress. In her spare time, she sang in a popular cabaret, then became a performer, singing between star acts in a Moulins Pavilion, La Rotonde. It was there she earned the name Coco, meaning 'Kept Woman,' after often singing the song 'Who Has Seen Coco?' Being young, beautiful, and respectful, she was adored by many.

In 1906, Coco worked in Vichy, a spa resort town with concert halls and theaters, where she hoped to become a famous performer. Unfortunately, her singing voice did not meet theater requirements, and so, she returned to La Rotonde, where she soon met Etienne

Balsan, an ex-cavalry officer and textile manufacturing heir. They fell in love, and for three years she enjoyed an extravagant lifestyle.

In 1908, she met Captain Arthur Edward Capel from the wealthy English upper class, who sent her to an apartment in Paris and financed her first boutique, as she had by this time become well-known for her hat designs, which were worn and modeled by famous theater actress Gabriella Dorziat.

In 1913, she created an exclusive and deluxe leisure and sporting clothing line in Deauville, which was modeled through the streets by her sister, aunt, and eventually, by other influential women.

In 1915, after great success in Deauville, she opened another store in Biarritz, opposite a casino. It was there her success became notable. By the year 1918, her financial success allowed her to buy an office in Paris, 31 Rue Cambon, and in 1919, she was officially registered as a couturière.

In 1920, she provided living quarters and financial assistance to the Stravinsky family of the Ballet Russes, which saw her turn to designing the company's dance costumes, as well. By 1921, Coco was producing and selling clothing, hats, and accessories, and by 1927, she'd expanded to offer jewelry and fragrances, too, and now owned five properties on the Rue Cambon.

It was during this time, in 1924, that she met the Wertheimer brothers, and together, they created Parfums Chanel, with the brothers financing the production, marketing, and distribution of the famous brand, Chanel No. 5. This was when she first faced a struggle, as she did not agree with their arrangements. However, Coco persevered for twenty years to gain full control of the company, and, in time, her demands were met.

In 1931, she was approached by Samuel Goldwyn, the famous film producer, who gave her one million dollars—these days equivalent to roughly seventy-five million dollars—to travel to Hollywood twice a year to design costumes for his stars. By 1935, the Chanel Company had four thousand employees, but it was also around this time that her 'boyish' style of clothing lost popularity as rival designer Elsa Schiaparelli joined the scene, with her surrealist styles gaining far more attention.

It was not long before Coco decided she did not enjoy Hollywood's film business, and so, by 1939, she turned to creating costumes for French films instead. This was a short-lived endeavor, however, due to the outbreak of World War II. Coco let go of her four thousand workers, which she saw as both necessary and, in a sense, deserved, because prior to this, they had chosen to strike for higher pay. Changes brought on by war also saw her finding a retreat in Switzerland, where she lived for a number of years.

During the war, Coco was involved in a number of political activities along with elite members of society. There was much controversy around her involvements, which ultimately led to her closing her couture house for fifteen years. In 1954, she returned to France and re-entered the fashion world, succeeding despite fierce competition.

On January 9th, 1971, now eighty-seven-years-old, Coco went out for a scenic drive, then she returned home to her room at the Hotel Ritz, Paris, feeling unwell. She passed away on Sunday 10th.

In 2022, the Chanel brand value worldwide was estimated at 15.3 billion dollars. Indeed, her unique styles, brand, and legacy live on.

Coco's Motivation

Perhaps one of the most accurate descriptions for Coco Chanel's personality was given by Sidonie-Gabrielle Colette, a French author, who stated, "*If every human face bears a resemblance to some animal, then Mademoiselle Chanel is a small black bull. That tuft of curly black hair, the attribute of bull-calves, falls over her brow all the way to the eyelids and dances with every manoeuvre of her head.*" [9]

Misia Sert of the Bohemian elite in Paris was one of Coco's closest friends. She stated that she adored Coco due to, '*Her genius, lethal wit, sarcasm, and maniacal destructiveness, which intrigued and appalled everyone.*'[10]

For instance, when the Duke of Westminster queried if she'd have his hand in marriage, Coco stated, "*There have been several Duchesses of Westminster. There is only one Chanel.*"[11]

Perhaps Coco's adaptation of the masculine style was a reflection of her tomboy-like personality, and perhaps it was her understanding of the masculine that led her to become such a fierce pioneer, entrepreneur, and competitor in the fashion industry. Her traits were not only seen through her designs, but also through her pastimes, which included horse-riding, golf, skiing, yachting, and fishing.

Coco herself stated, "*I invented the sports dress for myself; not because other women played sports, but because I did. I didn't go out because I needed to design dresses, I designed dresses precisely because I went out, because I lived, for myself, the life of the century.*"[12]

Certainly, she was neither shy, nor scared of those in power, and she did not hesitate to face controversy in order to make it to the top. However, she would have needed to be deeply respectful to others, so as not to be seen as a lunatic worthy of condemnation, in order to be as outspoken as she was. We must remember that, in those days, women who spoke out against or showed disrespect for men in power were often seen as troublemakers if not stark-raving mad. And so, to remain out of trouble, she would have needed to treat authorities with the utmost honor and integrity, while maintaining a relationship dynamic of equality.

It could be that having lost her mother early in life and being left in an orphanage were what led her to develop the motivation she had, which saw her challenging men, although respectfully, to preserve her legacy and place in the world. Caregivers at orphanages back then were often underpaid and demanded respect, using physical punishment to enforce desired behaviors, and so it is likely she learned a great deal about how to best approach authority there.

Known as a formidable businesswoman, the first of her kind to build an independent and international company, it seems her instincts never failed her. This suggests that with each decision she made, she must have felt some certainty she was doing the right thing. Indeed, she likely seldom experienced self-doubt or pondered upon thoughts of defeat—at least, not openly so—not even in her final days.

Coco was self-driven, self-motivated, understood the need for self-sufficiency as a way to succeed in life, and she never backed down on what she believed. Being highly creative, having made long-lasting friendships with avant-garde artists such as Salvador Dali, she was able to think outside the box, to find solutions to the challenges which came her way.

Perhaps she did not fear death or pain, and she did not lack conviction in her own powers, so she often walked where angels fear to tread.

Writer Paul Morand in his book *The Allure of Chanel* stated, "*She, by some sort of miracle, operated in fashion by following rules that seemed only to apply to painters, musicians, and poets. She imposed the invisible; she imposed the nobility of silence on the furore of high society.*"[13]

She was also considered by poet Jean Cocteau as being, '*An artist among artists.*'

While, in the past, some have said that the dog-eat-dog business world is one meant for men only, Coco proved otherwise, showing that, although the world of business and entrepreneurship could once be considered a man's world, '*. . . it don't mean nothin' without a woman or a girl.*'

How Coco Changed the World for Women

In a time when women were, in most cases, seen only as objects of beauty, caregivers, and mothers, Coco adopted a masculine style that saw her become one of the world's best-known businesswomen.

She had little to no fear, understood the need to respect those in power, and likely felt she had been left to raise herself emotionally. Not wanting to be seen as a burden to society or 'poor' after having been abandoned by her father, she developed an 'all or nothing' character, realizing that if she didn't save herself, no one else would do it for her.

Becoming trusted and respected by members of the elite for her bullish attitude may have grown from her not having an influential family behind her or an inheritance that allowed her to finance her future. She used her personality and inner strength, her daringness, her 'take it or leave it' approach to business to achieve what she did. She chose her word over the words of others; she trusted her instincts and maintained her authenticity and integrity at every turn, never cowering or running away from adversity.

Perhaps she felt the consequences of not being strong and assertive would be detrimental to her ambitions; sitting back and waiting for respect, fame, and fortune to land in her lap was not an option at all. Possibly, she considered death itself to be the only alternative to being outright, opinionated, and outlandish, and neither poverty nor death were paths she was willing to walk.

Indeed, she proved that women do have what it takes to succeed in a masculine-orientated world of business, and her fiery, brave persona continues to inspire other women around the world to this day.

Coco's Legacy

Without a doubt, Coco was one of the first female entrepreneurs and businesswomen able to 'flip' society into accepting that masculine traits could be adopted by the feminine; that women were no less than men, and they, too, should be allowed to feel comfortable in their daily lives, without living only to serve as caregivers and objects of aesthetic beauty.

At a time when women were seen as second best, she made it clear they are not to be undermined, and that anything a man can have and do, a woman should be allowed to have and do as well.

Women's worth was amplified through her choices and actions. Her boldness and lack of fear put her on par with the men, and as she was able to maintain this persona, so was she able to gain the confidence and trust of men.

Perhaps the quote found in *Harper's Bazaar* magazine best explains the legacy she left behind: "*The woman who hasn't at least one Chanel is hopelessly out of fashion.*"[14]

What Can We Learn from Coco's Story?

Above all, it can be said that Coco's bravery and tenacity were traits which saw her become a powerhouse in the fashion industry, an industry which, prior to her entrance, was dominated by men. It is also noteworthy that once the designs of men made a comeback, she grew quite upset at their being allowed to decide which fashions should be worn by women—this notion was in turn supported by other women as well, and she grew a following of important women in society who backed her claims and ideas.

Never afraid to make her opinions known, Coco's outspokenness is a value women can adopt today, yet it is important to keep in mind that respect is only ever given to those who earn and deserve it. While she always said what she wanted, she did so while being careful not to overstep the marks laid down by the businessmen she was forced to deal with. While she played on their turf, she still treated them with dignity, through a focused intellect and by being committed to her cause.

Having a way with words, which enabled her to present her points in ways seen as acceptable, her arguments were always valid. Her visions were new and, therefore, possible, as they'd not been practiced before, and her aim to bring balance and equality between the masculine and feminine was achieved.

What we can learn from Coco is that we should never doubt our ability to present and drive ideas we are passionate about to others, as long as we do so in ways which don't diminish their authority or dismiss their ideals. She always respected 'the rules' and avoided trickery or manipulation, knowing full well the consequences of both in an elite world.

She gathered support from others through simply being herself, and she became an inspiration to many women who also felt that equality between men and women was lacking, and that women should be granted 'the talking stick' from time to time, especially when it concerned their own well-being and lifestyle.

She paced herself and grew bolder with each of her accomplishments, never falling behind the line she set for herself. Each day for her was another opportunity to expand her influence without treading on the toes of those who could easily have seen her punished. It was her authenticity they admired the most, and for being authentic, she received the respect she both desired and deserved, perhaps thereby surpassing the achievements of any woman before her.

Olive Ann Beech

1903 - 1993

"If you want something, you can do it."
– Olive Ann Beech

Who Was Olive?

Olive Ann Beech (born Olive Ann Mellor) was born in Waverly, Franklin, on 25th September, 1903. As a young girl, she moved with her family to Paola, Kansas, where she was given the responsibility of writing the family's checks to pay bills, and she also had her own bank account.

In 1917, they moved again, this time to Wichita, Kansas. There, she was allowed to attend the American Secretarial and Business College, without having to attend high school first. At college she studied bookkeeping and stenography. She completed her studies at age eighteen, and then worked for an electrical contracting firm in Augusta, Kansas.

Between 1924 and 1925, she was hired by the Travel Manufacturing Company as an office secretary and bookkeeper. She was then promoted to office manager and secretary to Walter Beech, one of the founders of Travel Air. Travel Air then merged with the Curtis-Wright Corporation in 1929. Walter took up his position as president of the company and moved to New York, where Olive eventually joined him, and they married in February of 1930. Walter and Olive had two girls, with the second-born arriving almost a decade later.

During the Great Depression in 1932, they returned to Wichita and created the Beech Aircraft Company, with Walter as president and

Olive as secretary-treasurer. Their intention was to build the finest airplanes in the world.

The first plane built by the company was the Model 17 Staggerwing. Olive thought a great way to boost sales of the aircraft was to have a female pilot, Louise Thaden, take part in the 1936 Transcontinental Bendix Trophy Race. Louise went on to win the race over some of the nation's top male pilots. At the same time, Olive became a member of the board of directors for the company.

World War II offered the opportunity for the Beech Aircraft Company, and it converted some of its planes to be used by the military.

In 1940, Walter fell ill, and Olive assumed further personal responsibility in obtaining financing for the company. Most of her initial work at this time was done from her hospital bed, after having given birth to their second daughter, while Walter was cared for in the same hospital.

She then assumed leadership of the company and secured a loan of $83,000,000 in order to expand the production of the Staggerwing and the Twin Beech aircraft. Under her management, the Beech Aircraft Company made over 7,400 planes, supplying 90% of the planes used for training American bombardiers and navigators. Such success resulted in the company being awarded five Army-Navy E Awards.

In 1943, the *New York Times* selected Olive as one of America's Most Distinguished Women. She was also selected, twice, as one of the United States' top-ten businesswomen by *Fortune Magazine*.

In 1950, Walter passed away, leaving Olive as the president and chair of the board, as well as the first woman in the world to lead a major aircraft company, and the first woman to lead a Fortune 500 company. The company would continue to make planes for both civilian use as well as the military. In 1951, Olive received the Woman of the Year award from the National Aeronautical Association of the US.

In 1956, under Olive's leadership, Beechcraft Travel Air was created, allowing new owners to pay for their purchases through the Beechcraft Acceptance Corporation. The company also played a role in supporting the United States' space exploration efforts by developing cryogenic systems for NASA. For a decade, Olive's company continued with innovations and plane production in the industry. With the introduction of the Jet Age, Olive chose rather to remain focused on propeller planes. She also put much effort toward preparing her nephew, Frank Hedrick, for eventual leadership of the company.

Olive ran the business for eighteen years, and became known as the First Lady and Queen of American aviation. With the wealth she earned through the company, she also became a patron to various art groups and funded both local and state-wide scholarships. By 1965, her company had generated $164 million in revenue and $8.7 million in profit.

In 1968, Olive handed the presidency of the company over to her nephew, Frank, while she stayed on as chairman of the board. After great success, the company was sold for $800 million to the Raytheon Company in 1980, where Olive remained on the board, and by 1982, she and Frank retired from the business altogether.

In 1980, Olive was awarded the Wright Brothers Memorial Trophy by the US National Aeronautic Association for her contributions to the aviation industry. Indeed, this is the highest honor awarded by the organization.

Once retired, Olive went on to contribute to various civic and philanthropic projects, greatly supporting her church, as well as the Wichita Art Association, and the Soroptimist International of Wichita.

At age ninety, life began to slow down for Olive. On July 6th of 1993, at her home in Eastborough, Kansas, Olive passed away quietly in her sleep. She was buried alongside Walter at the Old Mission Mausoleum in Wichita, Kansas.

She will forever be remembered as the Queen of American Aviation, as well as one of the world's most successful businesswomen.

Olive's Motivation

Having understood how money works from a very early age, Olive always paid detailed attention to costs, gains, and losses in regard to financial matters. And she was very good at it. Handling a company's finances is an art, for sure, and she was one of the very few who could balance books and suggest routes to profitable success with ease.

One of the mottos she lived by was: "*If you want something, you can do it.*" This clearly depicts her determined and motivated spirit. Whatever she wanted to achieve, she would find a way. If there was no immediately obvious way, she would continue with her current formulas, while still keeping an open mind, looking for possible clues that could lead to finding a viable path. She knew better than to let go of the 'satisfactory' in search of the 'extraordinary,' understanding that 'satisfactory' at least pays the bills.

An example of this was when Olive decided to continue with producing turboprop planes, as opposed to following the latest hype or trend, which was the production of jets. When *Forbes Magazine* asked her if she would enter the jet production industry, Olive replied, "*We will when it is compatible with our other activities. Slowly we go.*" She did this despite risking losing potential profits from following the production trend for jet planes.

Olive only surrounded herself with '*people who like to find ways to do things, not tell me it can't be done.*' This said a lot about her motivation, too: if she set out to achieve something, she would not fall prey to doubt through others telling her what she wanted to achieve was impossible. If she saw it as possible, it was.

Olive was perhaps faced with doubt from male partners more often than any other woman in any other industry. Very few of them believed she could handle a leadership position in an aviation company. But, of course, she proved them wrong. This made her a role model to many other women in male-dominated industries, and in fact, she often advocated for women in business.

Olive seldom involved herself with others' personal matters. She was business-minded and served her company's goals with aplomb. This suggests she was very focused, and perhaps also a little stoic, in the sense that she knew refraining from involvement in emotional matters was safest, as a way to keep pace and prevent loss of time in achieving her goals.

She did not let others make choices for her, not even her husband, Walter. They would make choices together and seldom argued; debate was best. With her never-give-up attitude, she accepted failures easily, seeing them only as growing pains or lessons to be learned. She believed error should never be seen as the end, but rather as part of progress toward the ultimate goal.

Olive's motivation came from her ability to work with mathematics and numbers, in the sense that, just as numbers have an order, so do processes leading to success. If one follows a working formula, like the numerical system, success should be the result. But, of course, not all equations work out at first. And so, if at first you don't succeed, try and try again.

How Olive Changed the World for Women

Words used to describe Olive's personality were always positive when coming from those who truly knew her. She was seen as, 'astute, imperious, and impeccably tailored,' a 'change-maker,' a 'figure of grace, strength, and determination.'

As one of the aerospace industry's most successful businesswomen, through becoming the co-founder, president, and chairwoman of the Beech Aircraft Corporation, she won more awards, honorary appointments, and special citations than any other woman in aviation history.

Perhaps it was Olive's way with numbers that left men around her baffled. She had great talent with regards to financial matters, matters which professional men would usually hire helping hands to address, as they did not have the capacity to do it themselves. Having proven herself time and time again in this area of business, the men might have looked at her as some kind of genius—always correct in her equations, even saving the men some money where possible, certainly never making mistakes that would cost them.

Businessmen would have seen this as some kind of 'gift,' and those who worked with her valued her superiority in this regard. And so, we can see that Olive changed the world for women by showing men that her intelligence and way of thinking were valuable assets that should never be overlooked in the business world.

In this way, she changed the perception many men had of women at the time, steering their judgment away from the norm—that women should remain at home with their children—and towards the idea that women can be not only as intelligent as men, but even more so!

Olive's Legacy

Olive Ann Beech was awarded accolades so many times throughout her life, it can be difficult to keep count. Besides being termed the First lady of Aviation and the Queen of Aviation, she was recognized, even after her death, in the following ways (among others):

1. Olive was handed the National Aeronautic Association's Wright Brothers Memorial Trophy in 1980 for five decades of outstanding leadership in the development of general aviation, '*In recognition of significant public service of enduring value to aviation in the United States.*' She was the very first woman to ever be handed this award.

2. In 1980, Olive was given the 'Sands of Time' Kitty Hawk Civilian Award at the Wright Brothers Banquet of the Los Angeles Chamber of Commerce. She and Walter were the second couple to be added to the Aviation Hall of Fame, with the first being Charles and Anne Lindbergh.

3. In 1994, Olive was added to the Women in Aviation International Pioneer Hall of Fame.

4. In 1995, she was added to the International Air and Space Hall of Fame, at the well-known San Diego Air and Space Museum.

5. In 2013, alongside Walter, she was listed as one of the fifty-one 'Heroes of Aviation' (at number thirty-one) selected by *Flying Magazine*.

Another honor includes the 75th Anniversary Special Addition Beechcraft Bonanza G36, having been inspired by 'Mrs. Beech Blue,' a custom color Olive often wore and loved, after having been introduced to it by fashion designer Oleg Cassini. Just about everything she owned, dresses, suits, furniture, cars, as well as the interiors of her personal planes, featured this shade of blue. This was seen as a tribute to her strength, vision, and pioneering leadership.

What Can We Learn from Olive's Story?

Perhaps the most important lesson we can learn from Olive is the value of 'momentum.' When a formula works, you do not put an end to it until a new and alternative formula is shown to work better.

She not only dealt with and secured matters in the present, but she also dedicated a fair amount of her time daily to planning for the future. Because she was good with numbers, she was also timely and trustworthy in meeting deadlines on time. This is extremely important in a start-up or young business (also in an established one, mind you). Deadlines must be met, with goods or services presented at the appointed time, and never late, at least, not without fair reason.

Olive was often tempted to explore new plane production opportunities, but she knew better than to abandon projects that were currently providing income to take unproven chances. She was not a chance-taker, and clearly preferred the calculated, tested approach. She was meticulous about effective communication, avoiding misunderstandings at all costs. Everything had to be clear to her, as can be seen by her constantly referring to drawings created by chief engineers of the workings of particular planes.

Olive's path was one of simplicity. She knew there is never any need to complicate matters, especially not when just about all issues can be broken down into their respective parts, to see how they work together for the greater whole. She was also highly adaptive, and even went on to provide manufactured products like corn harvesters, cotton pickers, washing machines, and even pie plates!

Because of the way her brain worked, in analytical order and according to some form of a mathematical formula, she was able to always come to the best conclusion to any problems her company faced. And in this way, she boggled the minds of men for many years—with her sheer intelligence.

Pauline Trigère

1908 - 2002

"***You have to make things functional, but that doesn't mean they can't be attractive.***" - Pauline Trigère

Who Was Pauline?

Pauline Trigère was born on November 4th, 1908, in Paris, France. Her father was a tailor and her mother a dressmaker. By age ten, Pauline was a seamstress helping her mother, and designed her first dress in her early teens.

In truth, Pauline had wanted to venture into the field of medicine and become a surgeon, but her father would not allow her to pursue this path.

She completed her studies at the Victor Hugo College in Issy-Les-Moulineaux, near Paris, then went on to work in a salon, Martial et Armand, in Place Vendome. There, she learned to design and make clothing for women, and she did very well.

This was where she also met her husband, Lazar Radley, in 1929. Lazar was also a tailor, and together, they had two sons. As the threat of World War II began to present complications in 1936, the family left Paris for Argentina but decided to make their way to New York City first. Pauline did not see the United States as being her end destination, but they would ultimately open a family tailoring business there.

While Pauline did her best and put her efforts towards making the business a success, it was not enough, and she began working for designers Ben Gershal and then Travis Banton at Hattie Carnegie. Lazar, however, was adamant he did not want her to work; she should remain at home with the children instead. Pauline did not agree with this at all, and the couple divorced.

Determined to survive and succeed with her two children, Pauline sold a pair of her diamond earrings for money to keep her going, and then turned to her brother, Robert. He helped her to launch her first collection of eleven dresses in 1942, by showing them to a branch of American department store executives, who gladly purchased them.

One year later, Pauline was able to open Trigère Inc., with just over a dozen dresses which she placed in various stores across the country. Her designs were simple, and she loved working with wool fabrics, for which she became famous, designing and producing everything from coats to evening dresses. In fact, it can be said that Pauline was a pioneer in the cotton and wool fabric clothing industries, becoming well-known for garments such as the reversible coat, the mobile collar, the spiral jacket, and the sleeveless coat.

In 1949, Pauline received her first award, the Coty Award, which was seen as one of the most prestigious awards in the American fashion industry at the time. She would go on to receive two more of these awards and was added to the Coty Fashion Hall of Fame in 1959.

During the 1950s, she also added extra flair to her clothing lines by designing costume jewelry that complimented her unique and exquisite designs.

Pauline became so well-known, she began to design dresses for women such as the Duchess of Windsor, Elizabeth Taylor, Grace Kelly, Jacqueline Kennedy Onassis, Bette Davis, and also Meryl Streep, who wore one of her designs when she accepted her first Oscar award in 1979. This was a very special moment for Pauline, and proved her worth as a designer.

By 1958, Pauline earned in the region of $2 million yearly, owning a few shops where she showcased her dresses and accessories. In the 1960s, her designs were featured in McCall's New York Designer collection of dress patterns, which served the home-sewing market, bringing style and elegance to those who could afford to make their own clothes if not the sale price from a boutique.

In 1961, she was the first designer to use an African American model, Beverly Valdes, during the civil rights era. This caused some stir, and even resulted in one retail company canceling their order. Pauline did not mind this too much, and stated, "*We won't miss them*!"

During the 1970s, Pauline began mentoring other young designers through lectures at the Fashion Institute of Technology, helping future designers to learn the intricacies of design and fashion.

While Pauline enjoyed a good life and became very successful, in 1994, she closed her showrooms and moved to smaller premises, where she concentrated more on her jewelry and scarf collections. This was mostly due to many of the companies Pauline sold her designs to declaring bankruptcy despite owing her money for her clothes they had sold. By this time, she was in her nineties, but had not lost her creative flair. Indeed, she went on to design a line of stylish and sophisticated walking sticks for seniors.

At the age of ninety-three, on February 13th, 2002, Pauline passed away in her home in Manhattan. Today, as Hollywood seems to revisit the glamor of the past, her designs of clothing and jewelry have become popular again, proving her unique styles to be timeless.

Pauline will always be remembered as having taken huge risks, being true to herself, and doing what she thought was best, regardless of societal norms.

Pauline's Motivation

Pauline was also considered a 'trailblazer' who did not hesitate to speak her mind and do things the way she wanted to.

She did not always have things her way, though. As mentioned before, in her earlier years, she had wanted to become a surgeon, but her father would not allow it. She enjoyed being a seamstress, but knew from a young age what it felt like to be restricted from following one's passion. This may have been one of the reasons why she did not hold back on her designs; she was determined not to be restricted again, nor had her ideas put aside due to someone else's views.

Pauline faced such restriction again once she was married, too, with her husband deciding she should not work but rather stay home with the children. Between her father and first husband, neither of them truly supported her dreams for her future.

After her divorce, she was left with very little, and it is known that she sold a pair of her own diamond earrings just to keep food on the table. So, a larger part of her motivation at the start was also financial; she knew she would have to work efficiently if she wanted to succeed. She stated this herself: "*There was no drive because I wanted to become a great designer. I had two small children and a mother and we all had to eat. That's the drive I had.*"[15]

Through her designs, she promoted French fashion, and she remained close to this theme throughout her career. It is important to remember that, at that time, when a new era was starting after the war, there was much competition among designers. It was a make-or-break industry back then. Pauline did not make clothing to suit the masses, though. She made her dresses 'for' the masses, to help them feel unique, sophisticated, and comfortable, and by sticking with this outlook she became one of the most respected designers of her time.

She was also considered the first designer to use an African American woman to model her designs. This was a huge leap forward and not everyone agreed with it, due to widespread racism in America at the time. But she believed in beauty and wanted others to see that it does not only come in one color. This is one example of the boundaries she pushed during her career.

Pauline had a deep love for designing; even in her older years, once she'd retired, she continued to design walking sticks and other accessories for seniors. Being creative was important to her and finding the next 'new' thing was a challenge that inspired her to keep on creating, regardless of what others said or thought.

Through being strong-willed, focused, and thinking outside of the box, she achieved more than she set out to, and her dresses and designs are still loved today.

How Pauline Changed the World for Women

Pauline had a major impact on the fashion industry, not just in her time, but even today, her designs are a topic of discussion among modern designers, dressmakers, and fashion commentators. Among many of them, she is thought of as being the designer who marked the Era of Elegance.

Her career lasted for over fifty years, and over this time she continued to bring new, fresh, and exciting ideas to the world of fashion. In 1992, she was the only designer in the USA to have pursued the same career in design for this length of time. To celebrate the milestone achievement, a fashion show benefit event with six-hundred invited guests was held in her honor at the Fashion Institute of Technology in New York.

Pauline paved the way for other French female designers, helping them to feel confident enough to present new ideas and offer new designs, always breaking through the societal norm-driven perceptions of how fashion should be. Of course, she also helped unite women in fashion by breaking down racial barriers, something that had never been done before.

Today, her designs are still used and celebrated by fashion designers worldwide and are worn by a new generation of iconic women.

Pauline's Legacy

Pauline's financial success is a direct representation of the success of her designs. By 1958, annual sales at Trigère Inc. had reached over two million dollars. Known as a woman who never gave up, she was one of the few strong enough to turn unfortunate life events into opportunities or stepping-stones for her future. She always took a stand for what she believed in, and she certainly would never have made it as far as she did without having done so.

In 1993, Pauline was handed a Lifetime Achievement Award from the Council of Fashion Designers of America (CFDA). Not long after that, she was added to the New York Fashion Walk of Fame, and then, in

2001, she was handed the highest distinction for a French civilian, known as the French Legion of Honor.

Today, all of Pauline's personal papers are kept at the Brandeis University Archives and Special Collections Department, and more than thirty of her dresses and outfits are kept safely at the Kent State University Museum Designer Archives.

More recently, since 2021, Franklin Benjamin Elman continues to support the Trigére line by leading design in the Trigére Collection, maintaining the unique French style Pauline introduced and shared with the fashion world.

Besides her outfits and accessories, Pauline also created a line of perfume in 1973 known as Trigére, which can still be purchased today. Earlier, in the sixties, she also introduced and popularized the 'jumpsuit,' and was the first to design the 'Rhinestone Bra,' in 1967.

Her legacy lives on today as somewhat of a retro 'cult' that celebrates her label and name, with her designs and dresses available for purchase through the Trigére Online store as well as in selected fashion houses.

It is true that the French are known for adding elegance, grace, and uniqueness to the fashion industry, and perhaps it was Pauline who started this ball rolling.

What Can We Learn from Pauline's Story?

What Pauline needed most at the start of her career was support for her designs. Without her designs being seen by those trusted in the industry, it would have been very difficult for her to begin to be noticed.

She was fortunate enough to have learned the tricks of her trade at a young age, which shows us that if we have the opportunity in life to be taught a specific art or skill, this will only make us stronger and more learned in our future. It's not always that we have the desire to follow through with what we have been taught in our younger years, but learning a skill can provide a safety net when what we really want to do is not within our reach.

But we can also be stubborn as humans, and we should not put aside learned skills which can serve as tools and stepping stones towards our future. When offered opportunities in life to learn anything new, we should take them—especially if we show flair in a given field.

Pauline also teaches us that maintaining a steady pace as we begin our business, without giving up, can lead to worldwide success. And when we can earn a living from our learned skill or art, this can be a ticket to a prosperous life. When faced with adversity and struggle, we should see obstacles as just that—objects that can be moved or stepped over if we maintain the strength needed to face them in a competitive industry.

We should never step back from what we can be in order to please the masses. Often, by being brave and taking the steps needed to bring something new to the world, we can flourish, and even begin new waves of thought and action, as Pauline did when she decided to be the first to use an African American model to showcase her works.

We may face criticism and doubt from others at times. We may even lose customers or support from others when we dare to step out of our comfort zone, or even the comfort zone of society. But with a little conviction and sound reasoning behind our ideas, we can reach success on a scale that sees us overriding norms and, therefore, opening new doorways to new possibilities in the careers we choose to pursue.

In turn, this can lead us to becoming pioneers in our trade, and with that comes not only a bright future, but also a legacy that allows others to remember us as being the first to accomplish something no one has before.

Ruth Handler

1916 - 2002

> ***"Don't dwell on what happened, no matter how bad it was. Find something else to do. Find something to do to help others."*** - Ruth Handler

Who Was Ruth?

Ruth Handler (born as Ruth Marianna Mosko) was born on November 4th, 1916, in Denver, Colorado, and was the youngest of ten children. Her mother had health issues, and so Ruth was raised mostly by her older sister, Sarah (and her husband), from the age of six-months until she was nineteen.

While attending school, Ruth also grew up working in Sarah's drugstore, where she learned about business. She aspired to being a successful businesswoman from an early age.

In 1932, Ruth met an art student named Izzy (Elliot) Handler. They began a relationship, but during her sophomore year, Ruth went on vacation to Los Angeles, and, fortunately, was given a job with Paramount Studios. Still in love with Ruth, though, Izzy met up with her in California, and in 1938, they were married in Denver.

Izzy decided to make furniture, while Ruth worked at Paramount, first as a secretary, then as a stenographer. Izzy initially made his furniture from his garage at home, from two newly discovered kinds of plastics (at the time), known as Lucite and Plexiglas. Ruth suggested he start doing this commercially, and they began a furniture business.

Ruth left Paramount Pictures to help Izzy develop the business. But in 1945, at the end of World War II, not many people were buying furniture. Ruth then came up with the idea of creating toys out of the leftover plastic not consigned for making furniture. One of their friends, Harold 'Matt' Matson, was interested in the idea, and so, together, they formed the company Mattel (a combination of the name Matt and El for Elliot). Ruth was president of the company and also in charge of marketing and sales.

Together, they made the first 'Uke-A-Doodle,' a child-sized instrument that helped children to learn to play music creatively. With this toy being welcomed by the market, Ruth went on to think of more things they could make with the plastics from their company.

Ruth then landed a contract with the Douglas Aircraft Company, making die-cast models of the Douglas DC-3 airplane that Douglas Aircraft would give to their customers as Christmas gifts.

Whether she was inspired by dolls manufactured in Europe that looked like grown women (unlike 'baby' dolls), or by seeing her daughter making paper dolls, Ruth decided that girls would love to have a small doll they could take with them everywhere, and it would look like a real woman.

She then created the Barbie doll, which was, of course, named after her daughter, Barbara. The Mattel Company manufactured the dolls, which first premiered at the American Toy Fair, on March 9th, 1959, in New York City.

Barbie was an instant hit, and the Mattel Company sold over 350,000 dolls in their first year. With such success, the sponsors of the Mickey Mouse Club jumped at the opportunity to advertise the Barbie doll to children.

Not long after that, Barbie needed a boyfriend! And so, Ken was born, along with many other features added to the Barbie enterprise, such as a horse, car, and furniture, clothing, and more.

In 1970, Ruth was diagnosed with breast cancer. She underwent a mastectomy but could not find a breast prosthesis. And so, she decided to make her own. She teamed up with her friend, Peyton Massey, and together, they formed Ruthton Corp. They made a 'fake breast' which they called the 'Nearly Me.' It was accepted by many women and became popular when Betty Ford (first lady of the United States from 1974 to 1977) personally requested one be made for her.

Back to the Barbie doll: as much as it was loved by young girls, it was shunned by some mothers and folks who believed Barbie's perfect hourglass figure to be shaming to young girls, most of whom could not hope to meet the idealized standard of female beauty the doll appeared to embody. For this reason, Barbie underwent a few changes, but the Mattel Company did not stop the production of the Barbie doll and its accessories.

In 1974, Ruth was accused of financial fraud. Consequently, she resigned from Mattel in the same year. In 1978, after an investigation, she was, unfortunately, charged with fraud. She defended her actions, saying that cancer had made her become 'unfocused,' and that she may well have made mistakes as a result. This did not overshadow the success of the, by then, much-loved Barbie doll, however, and it is still a top seller to this day.

Ruth went on to develop cancer in her colon as well, and on April 27th, 2002, aged eighty-five, she passed away due to complications during surgery in California.

Ruth's Motivation

It's important to remember that Ruth was raised in a family that believed the idea of women working outside of the home was unusual. Her mother, after all, had ten children, and that was the only life she knew. Ruth wanted to be more than that. She believed she had to create her own income as well as contribute to her family's financial circumstances. And so, these aspects could be seen as the core of her motivation.

Ruth has been described as being creative, ruthless in her convictions, and highly adaptable to changing times. She would not settle for a simple life of earning a minimum wage and tips. Instead, she used her imagination to consider products for children (and, eventually, grown women). Then, with the skills she had developed in business through growing up working in her sister's drugstore, she found ways to make her ideas come to life. She was resourceful, in the sense that the toys were made from leftover plastics, which meant initial costs were kept low.

Perhaps one of the most notable achievements by Ruth was her effective marketing strategy. Barbie was sold with the promise of promoting the concept of positive role models for young girls, in a world where strong female role models were needed. Ruth stated, "*My whole philosophy of Barbie was that through the doll, the little girl could be anything she wanted to be. Barbie always represented the fact that a woman has choices.*" [16]

Indeed, both her creativity and her firm belief in her own creations were what saw her reach the level of success she did. Barbie was seen as having a social impact and also helped to revolutionize the toy industry. It is also important to note that it took Ruth three years to convince others that Barbie was a good product; nothing came to her overnight.

Beyond that, when Ruth created the 'Nearly Me' breast prosthetic, she stated, "*When I conceived Barbie, I believed it was important to a little girl's self-esteem to play with a doll that has breasts. Now I find it even more important to return that self-esteem to women who have lost theirs.*" [17]

She was a visionary marketer, unafraid to approach large advertising companies with her ideas. She took risks where necessary and, in turn, became seen as a game changer.

Overall, it was Ruth's creativity and determination to be more than just a hungry mouth to feed that led to her success. She believed anything was possible with the correct planning, and that many doors can be opened by simply knocking.

Her confidence, therefore, attributed greatly to her success which initially saw over five-thousand Japanese workers, with eight hundred in California, earning a living.

In this way, she made a valuable contribution to society and helped to change the lives of many for the better, despite the criticism she received for creating a doll that was physically unrealistic and seen by some as serving to dampen self-esteem in young girls. She, of course, as the creator, had the opposite perception.

She continued despite the criticism, and the market performance of the Barbie doll today—despite Ruth no longer being alive to see such continued success—is still very strong.

How Ruth Changed the World for Women

Perhaps the most significant impact Ruth had in the world for women was the creation of the 'Nearly Me,' the prosthetic breast for breast cancer patients. A very close second to that was what she perceived as the creation of a good role model for young girls which, in the time after the Second World War, was important as young girls did not have many independent women to look up to or aspire to emulate.

With her mother having been ill, she was raised by her sister, who also raised Ruth's other siblings. They all grew up without a mother figure, and so, they themselves had to learn from the outside world, from society. This is perhaps exactly what made Ruth as playful as she was when it came to her love for creating toys for kids. She also knew business is important if one is to survive on one's own.

Her determination to succeed, as with other successful entrepreneurial women, is what helped her achieve what she did. But also, she understood what was missing in life. Perhaps because her own childhood was mostly devoid of pleasures such as toys, she knew that what she had missed was what others needed, too.

She certainly was feminine in her persona and bringing attention to the need for girls to grow up with some kind of figure to help them decide who they wanted to be, how they wanted to dress and look, would have shaped many of the women alive today. In fact, Barbie still continues to inspire young girls, although that is a subject of debate, of course.

She worked well with men and offered them ideas they simply would not have been able to come up with on their own—because they were not women. She left her mark in the women's business world by introducing products for women, and she had to do so in a man's world, where men were mostly paying the bills.

She was a strong businesswoman with creative and playful ideas, showing us that business does not always have to be boring or about cars and home improvement products, airplanes or buildings. Women can bring products for women into the market, and they can succeed in doing so, especially if they have a strong sense for business.

Through her life, we can see she helped change the world for women. She made it clear that women and young girls simply were not being catered for in a way that would actually help them, via reflection and the simple understanding that women have different needs from men.

Ruth's Legacy

Besides designing and manufacturing a breast prosthetic that helped thousands of women around the world, Ruth also helped young girls to explore their own femininity. She was also a good, self-taught businesswoman—of course, with the help of her sister, as they ran her drugstore together in her younger years.

Once she had made enough profit in her business, the Mattel Company, she turned to philanthropy as well, giving back to those who needed it. She was recognized in a number of ways, including:

1. Woman of the Year in Business (*Los Angeles Times*).
2. Added to the Toy Industry Hall of Fame by the Toy Manufacturers of America.
3. Received the Volunteer Achievement Award from the American Cancer Society.
4. Became the first Woman of Distinction of the United Jewish Appeal.
5. Granted the Outstanding Businesswoman Award by the National Association of Accountants in 1961.
6. Granted the Outstanding Woman Award by the *Ladies Home Journal* in 1971.
7. Granted the Advertising Woman of the Year Award by Western States Advertising Agencies Association Brotherhood in 1972.

These were just a few of her achievements, but the legacy of Barbie is one that will likely remain for as long as the toy manufacturing industry exists. Mostly, the idea of being able to accessorize Barbie and friends, and kit them out with a house and furniture, allowed for the growth of female independence, providing young girls with a way to live out the 'luxury' lifestyle, even if it was unachievable in real life.

She will forever be remembered as the woman who created the 'compass' for young girls' fantasies of a fruitful and good life, which in turn helped to shift the perceptions of American society towards women.

What Can We Learn from Ruth's Story?

Ruth Handler teaches us that no idea is too small, and that a good idea when pursued can lead to a small fortune. She also teaches us that when our motives for creating a product are focused, we can better fill a gap which others might not have seen at the start.

Of course, there were many dolls to play with, back in the day. But she created one that was durable, easy to handle, movable, and portrayed the ideal, adult feminine figure. Most other dolls at the time were either baby dolls, promoting the value of traditional motherhood, or portrayed the feminine figure as being voluptuous or even disproportionate. It was this seemingly very small difference Ruth pursued, adding breasts, buttocks, and an hourglass figure that made the world of difference.

She, therefore, also teaches us that to stand out from the rest, we need to have something unique about our product, especially if we are providing a product to a market where similar items already exist.

Being creative, playful, and resourceful in adversity saw Ruth turning to toy manufacturing, and she may well have been inspired to create Barbie because she did not have the lovely things she wanted as a child. And so, we can learn through her life that creativity and imagination can be keys to success, in the sense that thinking out of the box and coming up with small differences in already existing markets helps products to stand out from the rest.

When starting a small business it is very important that the product we create is unique. It is also important for us to thoroughly enjoy what we do; otherwise, we will have no passion for our product, and will, therefore, not be able to sell it to anyone. If we don't truly love our product, why should anyone else?

While many entrepreneurs thrive on making things or providing services they see people need and cannot obtain, not many in Ruth's day were prepared or even financially equipped to make items that were deemed unnecessary, like toys. However, through creating her toys and watching their sales increase daily, Ruth proved that not all markets are as catered for as we think. In this way, we learn that no matter what idea you have for a product, you should try it out because it could be that the market for your product is actually very big—it's only that consumers don't yet know they could have and hold what it is you are willing to provide them with.

Joyce Chen

1917 - 1994

> ***"What's the basis for the issue, for the freedom I have?"***
> – Joyce Chen

Who Was Joyce?

Joyce Chen was born in Peking (Beijing), China, on September 14th, 1917. She is best known for her role in operating a number of well-known Chinese restaurants in Cambridge, Massachusetts, as well as popularizing Northern-style Chinese cuisine in the USA. She also invented and held the patent for the 'flat-bottomed wok with handle' (known more commonly as a stir-fry pan), developed the first line of Chinese stir-fry sauces within the US market, as well as coining the name 'Peking Raviolis' for her 'potstickers'.

Joyce was the youngest of nine children born to a high-ranking Qing Dynasty official during the Chinese Republican Era led by Sun Yat-sen. The family was wealthy enough to afford their own chef, but when that chef left to work for another official, Joyce's Uncle Li, Chinese ambassador to Russia at the time, her mother and governess took over cooking the family meals. Through watching and learning from them, Joyce was able to ultimately create a business for herself.

Throughout her early years, she enjoyed performing, and aged eighteen, she played the lead role in a Beijing Opera known as "White Snake." In 1942, Joyce married her husband, Thomas Chen, and together, they had two children. She worked as an insurance broker, which was not a common position for women in China at the time.

In 1949, as the political system in China veered towards Communism, the couple left Shanghai to settle in Cambridge, Massachusetts, where Thomas worked as an importer of fine art, while Joyce raised her children and ran the household. In 1952, she gave birth to their second son, Stephen.

It was in 1957, at a bake sale at Buckingham School in Cambridge, that she first realized her pumpkin cookies and Chinese eggrolls were a hit. She needed to adapt her recipe to suit the ingredients found in America, as the ingredients used in the original recipe were not available in the USA. Due to her cooked delights being loved by all, she chose to pursue cooking as a career.

In 1958, she opened her first restaurant at 617 Concord Avenue in Cambridge, which she simply called the Joyce Chen Restaurant. To boost sales, she introduced an all-you-can-eat buffet-style dinner on Tuesday and Wednesday nights, where customers could sample authentic Chinese dishes with 'real ingredients.' Indeed, Joyce refused to use dyes or colorings in her restaurants. She also addressed the translation issues between her language (Mandarin) and US English by introducing a simple numbering system, allowing English-speaking customers to request meals by numbers, not by name.

At the same time, she taught cooking at the Cambridge Centre for Adult Education, as well as at the Boston Centre for Adult Education. It is said that the waiting lists to attend her classes were extensive, as the education in Chinese cuisine she provided was unique.

In 1962, she published her first cookbook, *The Joyce Chen Cookbook*, which publishers considered too expensive to print in color, and so she printed it privately at her own expense. Joyce had already presold 6,000 cookbooks before the book itself had even been printed. Once popular, the book was taken on by a publishing house which printed and sold over 70,000 copies. The book featured a foreword written by Boston cardiologist Paul Dudley White, who praised the recipes for their healthy ingredients.

In 1966, she divorced Thomas, selling her first restaurant to him. He then changed the name of the restaurant to 'Osaka'. Upon the divorce, she changed her name back to her maiden name, Joyce Liao, but chose to use the Joyce Chen name for her business. Despite being a single mother now, with the assistance of her children, she opened a second restaurant in 1967, known as the Joyce Chen Small Eating Place.

Located perfectly between Harvard University and MIT in Central Square, it became a hotspot for those working and residing in the area (especially hackers). It was here she became best known for her soup dumplings, also known as Shao Long Bao. Also, during this time, she began her own televised cooking show called *Joyce Chen Cooks* (on NET, now known as PBS). Her shows were filmed on the same set as the well-known chef of French cuisine, Julia Child.

With great success there, she opened her third restaurant in 1969, at 500 Memorial Drive, Cambridge. It seated 500 people, but she had to close it in 1974 when the building was demolished to create dorms for MIT students. With these students having enjoyed Joyce's cooking, they fondly called their new dorms 'Joyce Chen Small Living Place' in memory of her establishment.

In 1971, she launched Joyce Chen Products, featuring high-quality cooking utensils.

In 1973, Joyce opened a fourth restaurant at 390 Rindge Avenue. The restaurant itself was secluded behind a garden featuring a single tree. Indeed, Joyce knew well the importance of location and setting when establishing her restaurants. This fourth restaurant operated for twenty-five years before closing in 1998.

In 1976, Joyce incurred an injury to her right hand, which required an operation. Shortly afterwards, she began to lose her memory, and in 1985 she was diagnosed with multi-infarct dementia. Her son, Stephen, took care of her at their home until 1992, when she was transferred to a nursing home in Lexington.

Sadly, at age 76, on August 23, 1994, Joyce passed away due to cardiac arrest, and was then laid to rest at Mount Auburn Cemetery in Cambridge Massachusetts.

Joyce's Motivation

Without a doubt, Joyce Chen was dedicated to health, refusing to use artificial chemicals, like unhealthy colorants, in her cooking. She also was able to find excellent substitutes for ingredients not then found in the USA, which meant she was focused on modeling her recipes as closely as possible to the real thing, without having to resort to synthetic ingredients.

Above all, however, Joyce noticed the gap in the market; the need for healthy, relatively inexpensive food for those who worked all day and perhaps had little income of their own. As an entrepreneur, she not only focused on her products, but also on the setting and venues for her restaurants. She was a clever, logical thinker who knew how to maximize aspects of her business through effective decisions like these.

It can't have been easy being a foreigner in the USA at the time she was there due to discrimination. But having no choice but to leave her homeland in search of a life she wanted to live with her family, she remained humble and kind, presenting herself as someone who certainly cared about peoples' health and the provision of cost-effective meals to the working and business community.

Expansion of her restaurants and products could not have happened without the initial motivation to fill a gap in the food market. Joyce went about her daily business seeking only opportunity, never doubting the possibilities, and always choosing wisely so as to maximize her business potential. Indeed, she is remembered fondly by those who knew her for being sweet and respectful, focused, and determined.

How Joyce Changed the World for Women

Not only did Joyce Chen change the health factor of fast-food-type cuisine, but she also overcame numerous personal obstacles in the sense that there certainly would have been an element of racism apparent in her time. Perhaps, through the laws she grew up with in her own country, she learned to respect authorities and display a persona that would never lead her into trouble—knowing well that in order to be successful in a masculine-driven business world, in a foreign country, women needed to show respect to the businessmen.

This is not something we see every day in our era; today, many women use assertion and aggression to get to where they want to be. But Joyce used her wisdom. And so, Joyce not only changed the world for women in business and entrepreneurship, but she also changed the world for foreign women in a new country, giving hope to others who wanted to set foot in the US and be productive there.

It is true that when we focus solely on our goals and how we can achieve them, as opposed to focusing on fame or profit, we tend to reach our targets that much quicker. We conserve our emotions in a world of entrepreneurship and business, never taking things personally, always looking at our product and business model as the perfect guide to determining our course of action.

One can only imagine this tiny woman facing a backlash from an unsatisfied customer; likely, she would have gently smiled and offered a discount or a second meal free. If the person accepted the free meal, it meant her product was indeed a success, and that the disgruntled customer had only wanted their money back. Surely, being as clever as she was, it was acts like these that helped her to prosper and succeed without having to face criticism or exclusion.

And so, women can learn from Joyce by observing the cheery, respectful, and logical personality that became the hallmark of her restaurants and TV shows.

Joyce's Legacy

Besides being remembered as a 'sweet little woman,' Joyce leaves behind a legacy through her accomplishments. Some of these include:

1. The introduction and popularization of Chinese authentic cuisine in the USA.

2. Introducing Chinese dumplings to the market through her very first restaurant, known simply as the 'Joyce Chen Restaurant.'

   Coming up with the now worldwide term 'Revs' or 'Peking

3. Raviolis,' referring to 'potstickers,' a type of small Chinese dumplings, in the Boston region.

4. Offering buffet-style dining that ensured her restaurant would at least cover costs on slow nights when not many folks had money to eat out.

5. Simplifying communication between Chinese and non-Chinese restaurant workers and customers by numbering menu items, as well as providing a single menu that could be read in both English and Chinese, known as the 'Americanised Version of Chinese Cuisine.'

6. Bringing polyethylene cutting boards, created by Sumitomo Bakelite, to the USA, as well as introducing, marketing, and patenting the 'flat-bottomed wok with handle' (stir-fry wok) in the USA, in 1970, which she called the 'Peking Wok.' She also sold other high-quality Chinese cooking utensils the American market had not seen before.

7. In 1984, being the first in the USA to produce and sell bottled Chinese sauces to supermarkets.

8. Motivating the growth of ethnic and unique restaurants at Cambridge, MA's Central Square.

9. Introducing Chinese cooking lessons in the early 1960s, at the Cambridge Adult Education Centre, as well as self-publishing her own color-print cookbook, which was then commercially published by the J.B. Lippincott Company.

10. Bringing and expanding awareness of Chinese cuisine to a large US audience through her TV show *Joyce Chen Cooks*, in 1967—the very first national show to feature an Asian host.

Today, Joyce's products still serve the masses as her son, Stephen, President of Joyce Chen Food Inc., continues to offer food and cooking-related products that include his mother's recipes, oils, sauces, condiments, and spices; some of which have been further developed to include certified kosher, gluten-free, lower sodium foods that do not feature added MSG.

Without Joyce, none of us might ever be able to say, "Hey, let's have Chinese tonight!"

What Can We Learn from Joyce's Story?

Perhaps the most important lessons we can learn through Joyce Chen's achievements are attention to detail, innovation, implementation, tenacity, and perseverance, along with respect, kindness, and perhaps even passiveness.

She also showed us that we don't need to stop at achieving our first goal; that we can put success under our belts and proceed to the next achievement, thus expanding on our abilities and, eventually, our profits. When we find a business model that works and is successful, there's no need to change the way we do things. We can see that model as the perfect guide to future success in the same area or industry.

She also teaches us that no idea is too mundane. Who would have thought that a flat-bottomed frying pan with a handle would be something that just about every household needs? So, through her story, we can see that when we have even tiny ideas which might not seem viable to others, we should follow our own intentions and not take their opinions too much to heart. Joyce shows us that if we see a gap in any market and know of a way to fill it to benefit others, we should pursue it, regardless of how simplistic or unnecessary the product or service might initially seem.

Bette Nesmith Graham

1924 - 1980

"***Women have to just keep on with their determination and be relentless. We have to not relent.***"
– Bette Nesmith Graham

Who Was Bette?

Bette Nesmith Graham was born as Bette Clair McMurry in Dallas, Texas, on March 23rd, 1924. Her childhood was normal, and she was educated but dropped out of high school at age seventeen to attend secretarial school. Although she never really aspired to being a secretary, meaning it was not specifically her childhood dream to become one, she was a strong woman who understood that a good job would secure her future.

Indeed, as a child, she enjoyed art and would often paint and draw pictures in her spare time. At age nineteen, she married her boyfriend, Warren Nesmith, and worked as a secretary while also attending night school to complete her GED. While she had dropped out of high school, she understood that a GED was important to her future, as well.

Not long after Warren left for service in the Second World War, she gave birth to their son, Michael, who actually grew up to be a guitarist for the famous band The Monkees.

However, when Warren returned from the war in 1946, the couple divorced, although she kept the Nesmith surname. By 1951, Bette was raising Michael alone while continuing her work as a secretary for the chairman of the board of Texas Bank and Trust.

With the introduction of electric typewriters and their soaring popularity in offices, secretaries often became frustrated at having to rewrite entire documents after making minor errors that obviously were not correctable with those machines.

Because she enjoyed painting, the idea came to her that when artists make a mistake on their canvasses, they can simply paint over them at no cost to time or the painting created thus far. And so, at home, she invented her own formula, similar to a thin white paint, which she could simply 'paint' over the errors made on the typewritten document. She'd then be able to type over the paint without the document having to be entirely rewritten.

Her original formula was made of tempera water-based paint she had used to decorate windows on festive occasions. She mixed her formula in a kitchen blender, tinting it to match the company's stationery.

Soon, other secretaries in the office saw how well her formula worked, and that the solution was accepted by the management. They asked her if she could make them some as well, and so she made her formula in bulk, then provided small bottles of the solution to other staff members who wanted it. She called it 'Mistake Out'.

The product Bette had made was soon in demand, and she realized she would do well to create a small business for herself from producing the formula and selling it those who needed it. And so, in 1956, from her own kitchen, she made the product, then hired her son and his friends to fill the bottles.

With her new business growing well, she began to put less effort into her work as a secretary at the office and, as a result, was fired. She was more than happy with this, as it gave her time to really focus solely on her Mistake Out business, which was proving to be more profitable than the salary she was earning as a secretary.

Over time, she went on to perfect and then patent her formula, calling it 'Liquid Paper'. In 1957, a magazine known as *The Office* published an article about the product, which resulted in the General Electric Company placing a large order.

With her business booming, she then met and married Robert Graham, a frozen-foods salesman, in 1962. He joined the business. By

1967, her formula had turned into a million-dollar enterprise, and they opened a new factory with twenty employees.

In 1975, Robert and Bette were divorced, yet for a time, she kept both names from her marriages: Nesmith Graham. In the same year, Bette propelled onward and moved her business to a 35,000-square-foot building in Dallas. Within a year, her formula was being sold in thirty-one countries around the world.

Bette was well-known for encouraging her employees to take part in making corporate decisions. She also set up a library at the factory, as well as a child-care center so her workers need not worry about their children while working.

Through running her own business and understanding the needs of women at work, she created two foundations to help women in need: The Gihon Foundation in 1976, and then the Bette Clair McMurray Foundation in 1978.

During this time, her ex-husband Robert was doing his best to remove Bette from the company they had created together. Fortunately, due to her having patented the original formula, she could prove it was her product from the start and was able to secure a deal with the Gillette Company in 1979 that would see her receiving royalties.

Just one year later, on May 12th, 1980, Bette suffered a stroke and passed away due to related complications, at the age of fifty-six.

Bette's story shows us that a simple idea designed to solve a problem in one's own life can certainly lead to great success.

Bette's Motivation

Bette never really knew her formula would become as successful as it continues to be today. But she seemed to know from a young age that to earn an income back in those days, she would have to work at a job that might not necessarily fulfill her creativity but would place food on the table. Knowing she would not be able to earn an income as an artist, which was what she really wanted to do, she used her logic and studied, in order to secure a good job.

She had a routine, and never saw marrying for money as being an option. Indeed, she faced financial struggles due to having to raise her son alone, and she would often become panic-stricken at not being able to make ends meet.

When it comes to the product she created, it was born from frustration—the frustration at wasting time on having to rewrite documents. At first, she did not even know if the documents would be accepted with 'paint' on them, but they were. So, she had to present the idea to her employer, in hopes he'd agree it worked well—which he did. She did not try to persuade anyone to use her formula; its benefits spoke for themselves.

She did not create her product to generate income at first. The income she derived from it was somewhat accidental, although in a good way. Once she realized the idea was a good one, she strived to perfect the formula so it would dry faster. Each time she sent a batch out to a customer, she would inform them of the tweaks she was working on to make it better, in hopes this would inspire them to try her newer formulas as well.

She had to promote and distribute her product herself, too, and would use her own money to visit companies to show them how it worked. This was likely when her motivation truly kicked in. She realized it was a good product and that it was worth paying from her own pocket to tell others about it—a product cannot sell if potential customers aren't aware it even exists. So, most of her time and personal income at the start was spent on 'show and tell' to companies which would eventually place orders in bulk. This took courage and determination. Fortunately, being routine-driven, she made it her priority and achieved what she needed to.

Her true challenge came when, after her divorce, her husband wanted her out of the company, or at least, did not want her to be allowed to make decisions for the company. She took everything in her stride and slowly fought for the right to her position in the company that she'd initially been allowed.

"*They wouldn't let me come on the premises or let anyone there have anything to do with me,*" [18]she stated. Her ex-husband also attempted to change the recipe for the formula, which would have excluded her in terms of royalties. All of this was stressful, obviously, as it certainly was Bette's invention and company, and the success was due to her efforts. Her ex-husband attempted to thrive on her hard work. However, she was successful in establishing her rights.

Bette also faced challenges upon realizing she needed to speed up the pace of production, as well as establish new premises where she could produce more and hire more employees. This she did on her own, and she had her own ideology for the company, which led to its success.

And so, Bette's core motivation was knowing she had a great product, and that with effort on her part, she could become financially successful. She persevered and became one of America's most successful inventors, entrepreneurs, and businesswomen.

How Bette Changed the World for Women

During the time when women were seen as subordinate to men, Bette had to fight a number of battles on her own. Besides a difficult divorce, she also struggled financially but did not want to be reliant on anyone. She had sufficient training when it came to business, not directly through having studied business, but she would have learned a great deal through being a secretary.

She seldom complained and chose to live an orderly lifestyle so as not to attract any negative attention. She was wise in doing so and gained respect from others due to her attitude and behavior.

With regards to the difficulties she had to deal with when her husband attempted to oust her from her own company, she would have needed to remain headstrong and stand by her conviction that the product and company were hers. This could not have been easy for any woman at that time, for society was male-dominated.

While Bette may not have had a major impact on the world as far as women's rights go, she did prove that with perseverance, respectful behavior, routine, and a clear plan as a map, women can overcome any challenges.

Beyond doing business with businessmen, Bette helped hundreds of women to live a better life, especially through the program or business model she created to ensure women were comfortable in the workplace. She ran her company through a combination of 'spirituality, egalitarianism, and pragmatism'. Her interest in Christian Science inspired the creation of her corporate 'statement of policy.' It included ethics, business philosophy, and focused on decentralized decision-making, while pursuing product perfection over profit.

She also believed that women certainly did have a place in business, and part of it was women's ability to bring nurturing and humanistic qualities to the masculine world of business. This is why she provided a greenbelt with fishpond, a library, and a childcare center at the company's headquarters.

Through her, men began to see that women do not only belong in the kitchen or at home with the kids, that feminine elements do belong in business, whether through determination and nurturing of a product, or through simple choices regarding the aesthetics of an office environment.

Bette's Legacy

Bette has been described as being courageous, bright, innovative, and persistent, having been one of the first women in history to prove that a woman could most certainly succeed well in the business world. She was also considered a self-proclaimed feminist.

She was very wealthy at the time of her passing. With two foundations in her name, her son, Michael, who received her fortune as inheritance, continued them, thus supporting and empowering women too.

As mentioned previously, these foundations were the Gihon Foundation, which gave financial assistance in the form of grants to promote women in the arts, and the Bette Claire McMurray Foundation which provided assistance to women in business, in the form of career guidance, scholarships, and financial education.

Today, the Gihon Program for the Performing Arts is unique in that it curates and produces live performances, with both new and established artists, that are presented to the public for free. The shows cover issues regarding culture, society, and the development of various civilizations. The artists are paid for their roles, whether as an actor or prop designer, and the aim of the shows is to reach out to other philanthropists to support similar issues and further assist society.

What Can We Learn from Bette's Story?

Today, we see a number of start-ups outsourcing production. For example, if someone wants a plush doll made, they will outsource production to a manufacturing company.

Bette did not have this option available to her, and initially, she had to physically produce her Liquid Paper formula on her own, in her kitchen, with her son and his friends to help her.

She promoted her product on her own, as well as distributed it where necessary. She would have had to travel to meetings in order to sell her products. These aspects make her a self-starter, and, therefore, an entrepreneur of her own company. Once she married, she had further assistance from her husband, Warren Graham. However, it would turn out that he would attempt to take the company from her despite it being her life's work.

She would have needed to remain strong during this time, as she fought to claim her rights to ownership. While she did eventually retire as president of the company, feeling it was being run well and did not necessarily need her anymore, she remained on the board, and was still obviously entitled to royalties on sales. This was a fight that would have required persistence and close observation, as we can be sure the businessmen and lawyers involved tried everything they could to keep her at bay and away from their profits.

Overall, through Bette's story, we learn that perseverance is key, and believing in your product and its ability to generate profit is important for success to be achieved. She also reminds us that we should never overlook 'small' inventions, those we make for ourselves without, at first, considering they could be beneficial to someone else.

If you have a product that fills a need, no matter how insignificant or 'unimportant' it may appear at first, you should consider pursuing it as an opportunity to create your own start-up. It may very well end up with you reaping profits and leaving behind your own legacy, as the first person to invent it.

Sometimes, the greatest ideas are the simplest.

Dame Anita Roddick

1942 – 2007

"Be courageous." - Dame Anita Roddick

Who Was Anita?

Anita Roddick, (Anita Lucia Perilli before marriage) was born in Littlehampton, West Sussex, England on October 23rd, 1942. Her parents were Italian immigrants who owned an eatery, in which Anita and her siblings would work after school and over weekends. Anita's parents divorced when she eight-years-old. Her childhood was not entirely stable, with her father having been an alcoholic. After their divorce, her mother married her father's cousin, who turned out to be Anita's true father, after all.

Anita loved drama and the arts, and after attending the Maude Allen Secondary Modern School for Girls, she applied to enter drama school, but her application was rejected. Perhaps a little unsure of what she really wanted to do in life, she decided to complete a teachers' training course at the Newtown Park College of Education in Bath, England, but ultimately ended up working (for a short while) at the morgue of the Paris office of the *International Herald Tribune*. Perhaps she used this job opportunity as a way to further study the human body.

Soon after this she moved to Switzerland, where she worked in the Women's Rights Department of the International Labour Organization.

Wanting to experience different cultures, she then moved on to work at a kibbutz in Israel, after which she traveled further to Tahiti, then

South Africa and Australia. It was during these travels that she spent much time with people who daily would rub their bodies in cocoa butter. Through communications with different people, she learned which extracts to add to a cocoa butter base, to make her own unique range of body care products.

In 1970, Anita married Gordon Roddick in Reno, Nevada, after having been together for six years and falling pregnant with their second child. Together, they ran a bed and breakfast lodging with an Italian health food restaurant.

However, it had always been Gordon's goal to ride on horseback from Buenos Aires through Argentina to New York, over a time span of eighteen months.

When Gordon left in 1975 on his quest, Anita returned to England, to her Brighton home, where she prepared her own moisturizers. In just one year, she opened her very first Body Shop in Brighton, although she had already opened one in Berkley, California by that time. Gordon had helped her to secure funding, and once the business was doing well, a local businessman named Ian McGlinn provided further funding and would have a 22% stake in the company.

Body Shops around the world are painted green, and there is an interesting reason why. Apparently, Anita had used green paint on the walls in her shop to hide the mold that grew on them!

Her products sold so well that they did not need to do any marketing. Some say it was Anita's wonderful personality that led to such success, with the *Telegraph* newspaper of London publishing an article saying: "*Loquacious, wacky, and opinionated, she was so far outside the normal businesswoman template that it was easy for her to attract free coverage.*"[19]

In 1978, Anita and Gordon launched their first franchise network outside of the UK, in Brussels, Belgium. By 1990, Anita was declared the fourth-richest woman in Britain.

Being compassionate, with a sincere love for nature and animals, Anita then began to help social-environmental causes focused on fair treatment of animals, the rain forests, debt relief for poor countries, voting rights, and cetaceans. She ran into a few issues due to this, though. One example was an incident in 1999, when she joined frontline protestors outside the World Trade Organization HQ to protest against the 'evils of global capitalism,' which confused some people because she was actually one of the richest women in the world at the time, with around 2000 shops spread out over 49 countries.

From there, she often found herself being considered hypocritical, as she would claim that her products were not tested on animals, yet—after investigation—it was discovered that some of the products she outsourced to make her own were animal tested.

Even after she stepped down as the Body Shop Company's co-chair, and the company was sold to the L'Oréal Company, environmentalists grew upset because the L'Oréal Company certainly did have a background in animal testing. While Anita had often been quoted when speaking out against the beauty industry's use of animal testing, she sold her own company to one which used those methods.

It turned out, however, that Anita considered herself to be somewhat of a 'Trojan Horse,' believing that if the larger, more profitable companies were to take control of hers, they would receive further criticism and would, therefore, have to alter their policies in order to match those of the Body Shop—according to public outcry.

Anita and Gordon then went on to create a non-profit organization known as the Anita Roddick Foundation, which she considered to be the best way to use the profits she had earned on the sale of the Body Shop.

In 2007, Anita told the public she had been diagnosed with hepatitis C in 2004 and had apparently contracted the illness while giving birth to her daughter in 1971. She underwent liver transplant surgery, but this did not stop her from fighting against industries she believed were causing the most harm.

Sadly, on September 10th, 2007, Anita experienced an excruciating headache and went to the hospital. It was discovered that she'd suffered a brain hemorrhage, and she passed away quietly at St. Richard's Hospital, Chichester.

Anita knew she had done a good job of raising her family, and that they were well-equipped to make it through life. Because of this, she left her estate to the charities she had supported in life instead of her family members. The estimated sum she left to the charities she chose was £51 million.

Anita's Motivation

As mentioned previously, Anita had a strong connection with nature, and also a deep drive to want to help where she could, with regards to environmental and human rights issues. Perhaps partly due to the somewhat abnormal circumstances of her parents and upbringing, she understood that different cultures worked differently and spent much of her time trying to understand the various cultures, to understand the divisions that separate humanity.

Long before the Body Shop was founded, Anita utilized what she'd learned regarding both history and English at teacher's training at college, as well as through her previous work experiences. She took what she'd learned and chose to travel, gaining more cultural and traditional experiences along the way—most of which were entirely different from her own British culture.

Once settled with her daughters, while Gordon completed his quest on horseback, she opened a small shop, where she sold the products she'd learned to make through her travels and cultural experiences. Gordon helped her to secure a $6,500 loan, and she contracted local herbalists to assist her in creating her cosmetics and creams. This resulted in the first Body Shop being opened to the public.

She did this mostly as a way to support herself and her daughters, never really knowing the company would become as big as it did. In a nutshell, her aim was to '*provide quality skincare products in refillable containers and sample sizes, all marketed with truth rather than hype*.'[20]

She was certainly, by this point, driven to shape ethical consumerism as well, and hers was one of the first companies to prohibit the practice of testing cosmetics on animals. Her company was also one of the first to promote 'fair trade' with developing countries.

An example of some of the movements she worked with at the start are Greenpeace and The Big Issue magazine, founded to help homeless people. In 1990, she founded 'Children on the Edge,' aiming to help disadvantaged children in Eastern Europe, Africa, and Asia.

She ultimately believed businesses could offer a form of moral leadership that would be more effective than religion or government. She showed this was possible through assigning moral-driven stories to each of her products, and through recycling at every turn. She stated that recycling bottles, for example, was not at first with the intention of being seen as environmentally friendly, but rather because they simply ran out of bottles at times. However, when other companies saw her do this, they followed suit, and around the world a message of conscious 'no-waste' production and consumerism was spread.

Anita never saw herself as being clever or cunning. Everything she did was based on logic; how to do things most effectively without causing harm on any level. It was never her intention to become famous or be seen as a powerful activist. Instead, her actions were natural and based on effective reasoning and resource conservation, which turned out to be very helpful in the implementation of practices that could slow or even eliminate harm through product manufacture.

Overall, she strived to understand life. Through discovering natural remedies for various ailments, she considered that a cocoa-butter-based product could help people when infused with different plants for different ailments. She then opened a shop and began very small, never assuming that her views and plans for her own business would have such an effect on the world. To her, it was merely a logical way to make money without hurting anyone.

When it turned out she was making a difference through her actions, she became widely spoken about, and, with the support she received, she felt stronger and was able to address the various issues she personally felt should be focused upon. She earned support through simple honesty.

Again, fame and fortune were never her goals. However, sticking to her plan to help where she could, while still earning some money to raise her family, was clearly the right thing to do. It has undoubtedly helped to shape the changes made to both industry and human consciousness regarding safeguarding the environment and human rights issues.

How Anita Changed the World for Women

Anita changed the world dramatically, not only for women but for all. She was neither a powerhouse nor someone with inherited influence. Rather, she was one small, conscientious lady who lived simply within her means. By providing products she thought were safe for the environment, she opened many doors that had before not even been seen in the business landscape before.

By following her heart and her own moral code, it was almost as though the changes she brought about were by accident. She never knew that others around the world were as focused on bringing awareness to the masses through creating environmentally friendly products, as she was. She never knew, and it certainly was not her initial aim, that she would be so quickly recognized and end up as a member of the Demos think-tank's Advisory Council, for example.

Anita never followed others' plans or programs. Instead, she was seemingly gifted with logic and creativity, which both served through her actions to show the world the underlying problems in society, the way consumerism was managed, and how and why certain products were manufactured the way they were.

She shows that by working from a moral-driven standpoint in life, you can achieve far more than what you initially expected; that when you work from the heart with the intention of making a difference, it's as though the Universe itself offers its support.

While she was quick-witted, humorous, and a problem solver, she had no malice whatsoever, and could never be likened to someone looking for 'get-rich-quick' schemes to obtain worldwide fame or recognition.

Anita changed the world for women through her display of focus and intention, allowing women to appear to the world as the true nurturers they are. She did not grow depressed or anxious in her work. Instead, she continued with her heartfelt purpose and, due to her understanding of life, culture, and social-environmental issues, was able to change the world.

Indeed, she proved that women are capable of bringing change through honesty, clarity, intention, drive, and kindness. No woman needs to be domineering, overpowering, or driven to break the glass ceiling. When we act from the heart, without massive gains as our objective, we often become supported.

Anita's Legacy

Anita's name and legacy will continue to live on for generations to come.

The executive director of Greenpeace, John Sauven, stated, "*She was an amazing inspiration to those around her—so ahead of the time when it came to issues of how business could be done in different ways. She was a true pioneer.*"[21]

Indeed, her achievements were many, and although she did not attempt to violently or illegally begin a revolution, she certainly had no problem with bringing important issues forward, as can be seen in her book *Take It Personally*, in which she encourages the end of exploitation of workers and children in underdeveloped countries.

A good way to understand Anita is to take a look at the core values of her socially responsible vision for the Body Shop. These are:

1. To raise awareness of and work against animal testing.
2. To support community trade as far as possible.
3. To activate self-esteem through providing environmentally friendly products that allow users to feel they are doing the right thing.
4. To defend human rights in working, lifestyle, and consumerism environments.
5. To protect our planet as far as possible.

She received countless awards, mentions, and honors as well. Some of these include:

1. The Veuve Clicquot Businesswoman of the Year in 1984.
2. Officer of the Order of the British Empire (OBE) in 1988.

3. An honorary doctorate from the University of Sussex in 1988.
4. The Center for Word Development Education's World Vision Award in 1991.
5. The Banksia Foundation's Australia Environmental Award in 1993.
6. The Mexican Environmental Achiever Award in 1993.
7. The National Audubon Society Medal, USA, in 1993.
8. The Botwinick Prize in Business Ethics, USA, in 1994.
9. The University of Michigan's Annual Business Leadership Award, USA, in 1994.
10. An honorary doctorate from the University of Victoria, Canada, in 1995.
11. The Women's Business Development Centre's first annual Woman Power Award, USA, in 1995.
12. The Women's Center's Leadership Award, USA, in 1996.

In 2005, the Shell Livewire survey of inspirational role models saw Anita in third place, just behind Richard Branson.

In 2006, she won the Spirit of the Rainforest Award from the Rainforest Action Network, for her contributions towards the inclusion of native tribes in the manufacture of products, as well as her efforts to preserve the forests from destruction.

David Holmes, a British podcast host and actor, put it well when he stated, "*She was a straight-down-the-line entrepreneur, yet she always used to say that she had never run a business in her life.*"[22]

Indeed, she did not study business at all, and can, therefore, only be seen as having been born with an entrepreneurial, problem-solving mind.

David also stated, "*Anita was always very generous with her time and was a charismatic and passionate leader who was completely principle-driven. She was the first person to make social responsibility part of company culture.*"[23]

What Can We Learn from Anita's Story?

Although she was loved by many, but not so much by certain industries, Anita achieved what she set out to without even having a plan of action in place.

Through this, we can clearly see that sometimes it is simply our perception of the way things should be that brings about change and success. When we do things in our own capacity without 'hype' and the need to set 'trends' or manipulate others through false claims to boost the chances of our product's success, it's often that we win simply through our initial intention to provide ourselves with something we need.

In turn, once others discover the benefits, they begin to acknowledge, accept, and then adopt a way of life based on the same principles that led to the invention and creation of the product in the first place.

Everything about Anita's products was conscious, from creation to production, to packaging and even distribution. The Body Shop products were not only 'nice' to use, they were the 'right' product to use.

In an article featured in *The Telegraph*, Anita was fondly described as, "*Highly likeable in many ways, though to some also extremely irritating.*"[24] Of course, when one is seen as doing good by one side, we can be sure that another sees it as destructive and getting in the way of what they want to do.

And so, Anita teaches us that continuing with our chosen path regardless of what others might say, or the obstacles they might attempt to throw in our way, we should always work from the heart, using facts instead of fancy sales talk.

Anita Roddick was one of the inspiring Leaders of Transformation in our time. She was a true pioneer of social responsibility, community building, environmental consciousness, and fair trade in the global business community.

Your Questions

Let's Answer Your Questions to Help You Feel Motivated

1. What kind of obstacles can young women entering the entrepreneurial world expect to face, and how can they overcome these obstacles without feeling demotivated?

In most cases, we find the stereotypical reactions that come with male-dominated industries; 'Does this woman really have the ability to make it in a male-dominated business world?' The answer to this is that women seemingly have a hidden secret power known as 'intuition,' and this often sees them making correct gut choices for their business.

Women tend to look more at obstacles and challenges that could present themselves, and they find ways to overcome them before they even appear. This 'prevention is better than cure' attitude found in motivated women is a key to success.

This could be considered a 'maternal' instinct, too, with the business being the 'baby' and the mother constantly keeping an eye out for threats, while, at the same time, nurturing and growing their business to be the best it can be.

To overcome the doubt others may have in you, it is simplest to see this doubt as 'just a minor obstacle' during your planning stages. When considering those who can help you to reach success, simply leave out anyone who does not believe in you or your project. Eliminate them from your thoughts so you do not create unwanted emotions. However, considering their opinions also helps you to find ways around these types of obstacles, and in doing so, you will be prepared for any doubtful comments you may face once your business starts rolling. The best way to overcome doubt is to prove those doubts to be unrestrictive.

Think of possible questions investors or customers may ask and have answers ready for them. Use your self-confidence to stay your course and continue to remind yourself that your goals are yours, not theirs—it's up to you to meet them, not others. Own your business and believe in it.

2. Where and How Do I Begin to Plan my Start-up or Small Business?

Parminder Vir OBE (Expert, African Entrepreneurship, Partnership Development and Mentorship, award-winning film and television producer) has the following to say, and it answers this question well:

"*We know that entrepreneurs are problem solvers. Where others see challenges, they see opportunities. If you are thinking of starting a business, you must first identify that opportunity then define the product, and/or service.*"

Consider what Parminder says, then ask yourself these questions:

1. What is the problem you are trying to solve?
2. Who exactly has this problem?
3. What is your solution?
4. Which features of your solution are new?
5. What will it cost to build these new features?
6. Which features of your solution already exist?
7. How can you exploit these existing features?
8. Are your users the same as your customers?

By answering questions like these, you should have a good base to start from. You can find Parminder Vir's profile on LinkedIn.

3. What Kind of Business Should I Start?

There is never any use in starting a business just for profit. If you do not have passion for your product, you will soon become tired or bored, even despondent. The product or service you want to sell should be one that makes you excited when you wake up each day; you should want to wake up just so you can 'get to work.' This is the feeling you should look for, this 'excitement.' Without such excitement and passion for your product or service, how can you expect anyone else to feel passionate about it?

Your new business should not cost an arm and a leg; it should not cost you much at all. Remember, in most cases you will have to pay your investor back in full or via profits, and if you borrow too much and your product does not sell, you will be left worse off than you were before you began.

Your product or service should be able to grow, in the sense that, for example, if you have made one t-shirt with the picture of the planet on its front side, you should foresee that you could possibly print the same emblem onto a journal, hat, coat, mug, or other items. You may even wish to write a book about the t-shirt and its meaning—as long as what you have started is expandable.

You should be a person who is also solution driven and willing to accept the opinions of others (even if you choose not to take them to heart). This means you should be a problem-solver, adaptable, and even a little changeable, especially in the business world, where you're sure to eventually come across those who want to oust your product in the name of competition. Be strong in your conviction and know absolutely everything there is to know about your service or product, so you are able to quickly overcome challenges as they arise, without having to slip into self-doubt.

You also must believe in your product or service, as without your faith in it, others won't have any at all. You will ideally sell your product due to its ability to fill a need in the person who may be interested in it. Because of this, you will need to know every benefit of your product or service inside out, so as to be able to assure others they are spending their money wisely, while fulfilling a need (or want) at the same time.

4. What Are the Biggest Challenges to Starting a Business?

According to *Forbes* magazine, some of the biggest challenges you can expect to face when starting your own business include the following:

1. Finding out what you're good at and thinking of a product or service that can best manifest your personal skills or perceptions, while serving a specific market.

2. Having to alter your business plan to better accommodate the needs of the market you choose to focus on, while still remaining unique.

3. Lack of cash flow or capital at any given point.

4. Maintaining a good pace throughout the initial stages, all the way through to success. Remember, success does not end at the first sale. Success comes with endurance and consistency.

5. Working even when you do not feel like working.

6. Learning to handle rejection and finding the inspiration and motivation to try and try again, as well as knowing when it's necessary to perhaps change something in your formula to better accommodate potential customers.

7. Finding good employees to assist you and making sure their motivation and determination, as well as their vision for the end goal, matches yours.

8. Knowing when and how to say 'no, thank you' professionally.

9. Effectively covering every aspect of your business, thus being able to 'wear many hats.'

10. Time management; you will need to learn it well, in order to achieve each of the steps you have laid down for yourself on your path to success, as well as maintaining a good work/life balance.

5. What Are Some of the Biggest Mistakes Made by Start-up Entrepreneurs?

When starting your own business, besides looking at others who have become successful, it can certainly help to observe mistakes made by others, as well. In this way, you can learn what not to do. Some of the common mistakes include:

1. Not securing enough funding to truly get your business off the ground as effectively as you should.

2. Expecting first-time success, in that you give up immediately after your first attempt fails, without nurturing the motivation and determination you need to stay the full course.

3. Overspending or cutting back on an expense that should rather have received more attention and funding. Ineffective budgeting can lead to failure.

4. Ignoring the quality of your service or product, or not accepting feedback that could improve it and make it more valuable.

5. Not placing enough effort into marketing and promotions. Keep in mind that no one will see your product or be able to form a positive opinion on it unless you present it to them well.

6. Not making changes fast enough if you find yourself selling a product in a competitive market. If even one small change can define your product from other similar products and make it more valuable to the consumer, you should make the change.

7. Entering a market without knowing your competition. It is important to ensure that your product or service has value over others, and you can only do this by observing your competitors.

8. Not securing contracts and addressing legal matters. Always read the small print, and always define your objectives clearly so as not to be misunderstood.

9. Not carefully selecting your team or screening those whom you consider to be employees. Make sure they are trustworthy, determined, focused, and have a good list of references or are able to prove their worth in your business.

10. Overpricing or under-pricing your product or service. It is good to incorporate a plan to introduce your product at a fair price in your marketing plan, and then set a timeline through which you can raise your pricing according to demand and the competitive market. This is the way with new products; introduce your product at a price that makes the consumer feel they have nothing to lose. As your product gains popularity and trust, you can raise the price to meet the competitive market, or if your product is deemed superior to competitors', you can charge a little more. Many people are willing to pay more for quality but will ignore high prices at the start without being given the opportunity to test the product.

6. Do I Need a Business Plan?

Most certainly! And without one you will not achieve much. When creating a plan, you will need to consider all the steps that need to be taken from the very start. This includes time management, product manufacture or timeline of service delivery, financial management and projections, marketing management, a promotions plan, and the incorporation of feedback.

When seeking funding, you cannot enter any meeting of this nature without a written plan. The plan does not need to be long. In fact, investors seldom have time to read long documents, and so you should open your business plan document with a point form list of what you will be providing, how you intend to provide it, when you intend to provide it, and—most importantly—how the investor will benefit from choosing to assist you.

7. How to Find a Good Name for Your Business?

Names for businesses are difficult to come up with. It is important to find a name that is not too long, so as to make it simpler for potential customers to find you in a search on the Internet, or to remember the name of your company.

The name you choose should suit your product in such a way that when someone mentions your company name, others will automatically know what it is you are selling.

Try not to add punctuation marks in your company name where possible, and also consider the spelling—if you're going to use an exotic name that is difficult to spell, this will also stand against you when potential customers cannot find you in a phone book or on the internet.

Brainstorming is the best way to choose a name. Once you have a list of around ten names, you can narrow it down with the help of friends and colleagues; a vote can work, of course.

8. How Can I Secure Funding for My New Business?

There are many books available, as well as articles on the Internet, that cover ways to apply for and secure funding. The following is a list of possible funding sources, or sources through which you could obtain funding with the right proposal:

1. Use your own money if you can. In this way, you will not owe anyone anything.

2. Make use of credit cards or a bank loan, although you will need to be 100% sure you will be able to pay back the money you spend, plus interest.

3. Ask friends and family members for support.

4. Consider 'Angel investors,' who, in most cases, can provide you with all the funding you'll need in return for shares in your business or convertible debt.

5. Consider the various crowdfunding websites available, but always be sure to read the small print to make sure you properly understand their requirements.

It will be important when asking for funding to have considered absolutely every cost that needs to be covered. The funding you get should cover you for at least the first seven months—you will also need to live and function effectively while you get your business off the ground; you might not necessarily be earning anything (let alone making any profit) at the start. Once you have worked out your costs and expenses, you should also include a small amount for 'miscellaneous' activities or items that may be unforeseen but will need funding.

9. List of Online Resources to Consider When Planning Your Start-up Business.

The following is a list of websites you can refer to when starting your own business.

www.AllBusiness.com
www.Inc.com
www.Entrepreneur.com
www.SBA.gov
www.Business.com
www.IRS.gov
SmallBusiness.FoxBusiness.com

10. How Can I Protect My Great Idea?

If you feel your idea is unique and you're afraid someone else may use it, you can patent your product or require anyone who reads any documentation about your project to sign an NDA—a Non-Disclosure Agreement—that prevents them from using your idea or sharing it with anyone else. In most cases, however, large investors have no intention of stealing your ideas; even if it is a good idea, they themselves will not have the time to implement your plan and will see more benefit in supporting you rather than going through the effort themselves.

Another good way to copyright your work is to have a state authority, or even a police official, sign your documents, which you can then send to yourself via the postal service in hard copy. The stamp and date on the envelope as well as the authority's signature can serve as proof that the initial idea was yours, should a competitor arrive after you've written your plan and claim it as their idea. The dates and stamps will prove the time and place where you first put your plan to paper, and it will be viable in court.

Conclusion

Your Road to Success Looks Bright!

In the world we live in today, with all its new norms, opportunities for success present themselves daily to those who are focused enough to see them. It is very seldom in life that fortune, fame, and respect land in our laps like leaves from a tree in fall.

Not much comes easily today, though it is true that successful business investors seek the most talented individuals to support. If your attitude is wrong, you will not be heard. If you have no plan, you will not be acknowledged. And if you have no respect, you will not be tolerated.

But there is a fine line between being over-confident and under-achieving in the business world. Indeed, the line that many young entrepreneurial women will walk today is thin and often erratic. If you see your goal as the horse you are riding, you'll need to be sure you feed, water, and exercise that horse frequently, remaining aware of any problems, like lameness, it may experience. You will always need to make time to consider solutions through sound thinking, often leaving emotion out of the picture, in order to tackle the more complicated tasks that often present themselves as obstacles.

While the stories you have read in this book are about women from years gone by, it was these women who paved the road to success for other women to follow after them. You may have noticed that most of them are fiercely individual and unique, developing and using their personality traits to get them to where they wanted to be.

When we walk a path of tenacity and focus, not much can stand in our way. When we make others feel calm and at ease in our presence, they listen more easily to what we have to say. When we achieve success, we do not stop there and sit back to relax for the rest of our lives. No, we find another goal to aim for; we choose to improve on and enhance our achieved goals and remain in a space where we're constantly considering new ideas that will serve to expand on our original ideas, either refining our products or plans of action, in order to offer the best we can in the fields we choose.

Being an entrepreneur is not for the faint of heart. There will be much rejection at the start for some, but because you already know this, you will likely have developed a personality trait that sees you overriding the negatives in search of the positives. To be realistic, if we consider the initial chances of success for a new start-up are one in ten, we must prepare ourselves for initial rejection or failure without taking it personally or emotionally.

When directing your grant request toward an investor, it will be very important to design a proposal that appears to meet the needs of the investor; if you can provide an idea and plan that seemingly makes the investor's life easier or will bring them greater profit, you should hit the mark and find funding without losing much.

When submitting proposals for funding, be sure to word your documents in ways that appeal to the specific investor. This means tweaking your original plan of action from time to time, in order to present to your investor the key they have been searching for.

This, along with a respectful, driven, and authentic personality should see you make that first deal which will introduce your product or ideas to the market, and lead to success for both you and your investor.

So, if you have an idea you feel could help the world or bring value to the lives of others, don't hesitate to get started on mapping out your plan of action, using the information provided throughout this book as your guide.

Here's wishing you nothing but success!

You got this!

Thank You

Thank you for reading this book!

If you would like to help authors like me, it would be very helpful if you would be kind enough to leave a review as it makes all the hard work worthwhile.

Many thanks, I very much appreciate it!

Read More

A fascinating and amusing collection of life accounts of great women adventurers to inspire teen girls and young women!

About the Author

Ariana Smith is a financial expert, entrepreneur, and writer. Her many years of professional and personal experience through motherhood have nurtured in her a passion for telling inspiring stories to children, teens, and young adults.

She is passionate about empowering young readers to embrace their own identities. Ariana believes in instilling timeless values through history and literature; her mission is to help young generations find their purpose and develop self-confidence and skills that will help them lead fulfilling lives doing what they love.

Ariana's books are written in simple and engaging language and can be read independently by children, teens, or their parents. Her work has proved especially valuable to young readers seeking to develop critical thinking skills.

When she's not writing, you will find Ariana reading, cooking, or spending time with her beloved husband and their three beautiful children.

Visit Ariana's website to learn more. Sign-up to her newsletter to stay connected and get her upcoming books for free!

www.ariana-smith.com

Ariana Smith

References

abcnews.go.com, Scandal tainted long career of Barbie's creator. abcnews.go.com/Business/story?id=6934823&page=1

ai-bees.io, Ruth Handler: Inventor Entrepreneur who Revolutionized the Toy Industry.
ai-bees.io/post/ruth-handler-inventor-entrepreneur-who-revolutionized-the-toy-industry

Biography of Madam C.J. Walker, American Entrepreneur.
thoughtco.com/madame-c-j-walker-1992677

biography.com, Coco Chanel.
biography.com/history-culture/coco-chanel

bookshop.org, Take it Personally.
bookshop.org/p/books/take-it-personally-anita-roddick/10700025

bostonglobe.com, Devra First on how Joyce Chen and Julia Child changed cooking forever.
bostonglobe.com/2022/03/03/special-projects/devra-first-how-joyce-chen-julia-child-changed-cooking-forever/

brandeis.edu, Pauline Trigère Papers.
brandeis.edu/library/archives/essays/special-collections/trigere.html

britannica.com, Olive Ann Beech.
britannica.com/biography/Olive-Ann-Beech

Britannica.com, Pauline Trigère.
britannica.com/biography/Pauline-Trigere

Bundles, A'Lelia (2001). On Her Own Ground: The Life and Times of Madam C. J. Walker. New York: Scribner.

Campbell, P. S. (1922). "Nostrum and Quack Evil". The Public Health Journal. 13 (9): 400-10. JSTOR 41972903. jstor.org/stable/41972903

cfda.com, Pauline Trigere.
cfda.com/members/profile/pauline-trigere

chanel.com, Coco in words - Liberated.
chanel.com/us/about-chanel/the-founder/

chanel.com, The History - 1931 Gabrielle Chanel in Hollywood.
chanel.com/us/about-chanel/the-history/1930/

Charles-Roux, Edmonde (1981). Chanel and Her World. London: Weidenfeld and Nicolson

cnbc.com, How inventing Liquid Paper got a secretary fired and then turned her into an exec worth $25 million.
cnbc.com/2018/07/19/inventing-liquid-paper-got-a-secretary-fired-and-then-made-her-rich.html

Coco Chanel | Biography, Fashion, Designs, Perfume. britannica.com.
britannica.com/biography/Coco-Chanel

digital.library.unt.edu, Oral History Interview with Bette Graham, April 2, 1980.
digital.library.unt.edu/ark:/67531/metadc1451175/

Elise Pinckney and Marvin R. Zahniser, eds., The Letterbook of Eliza Lucas Pinckney: Intriguing Letters by One of Colonial America's Most Accomplished Women, Eliza Lucas Pinckney, Columbia, South Carolina: University of South Carolina Press, 1972, Google Books. books.google.ee/books?id=VP8pMY1INfgC&redir_esc=y

Eliza Bio - Eliza Lucas Pinckney Chapter - NSDAR Honors and Legacy.
elizalucaspinckneynsdar.org/eliza-bio

encyclopedia.com, Chen, Joyce.
encyclopedia.com/humanities/encyclopedias-almanacs-transcripts-and-maps/chen-joyce

encyclopedia.com, Handler, Ruth Mosko.
encyclopedia.com/religion/encyclopedias-almanacs-transcripts-and-maps/ handler-ruth-mosko

encyclopedia.com, Pinkham, Lydia E. (1819-1883).
encyclopedia.com/women/encyclopedias-almanacs-transcripts-and-maps/pinkham-lydia-e-1819-1883

encyclopedia.com, Roddick, Anita.
encyclopedia.com/history/encyclopedias-almanacs-transcripts-and-maps/roddick-anita

entrepreneur.com, Anita Roddick.
entrepreneur.com/growing-a-business/anita-roddicks-biography/197688

express.co.uk, Coco Chanel's decade long affair with Duke of Westminster ended with proposal.
express.co.uk/celebrity-news/1657598/coco-chanel-relationship-scandal-duke-of-westminster-royal-proposal-denied-spt

ft.com, Gordon Roddick: My First Million.
ft.com/content/7600fac6-c581-11de-9b3b-00144feab49a

gihon.com, Biographical Sketch of Bette Graham.
gihon.com/about.php

historybyday.com, The Fragrance of WWII: Coco Chanel's Sinister Truth.
historybyday.com/pop-culture/the-fragrance-of-wwii-coco-chanels-sinister-truth/10

historycambridge.org, Savoring the Legacy of Joyce Chen.
historycambridge.org/articles/savoring-the-legacy-of-joyce-chen/

joycechenfoods.com, Rr. Paul Dudley White endorsed Joyce Chen's Recipes as 'good for the health'.
joycechenfoods.com/news/Preventative-Cardiology-Founder-Paul-Dudley-White-Endorsed-Joyce-Chens-Recipes

joycechenfoods.com, Savouring the Legacy of Joyce Chen - Her Story.
joycechenfoods.com/legacy/

jwa.org, Ruth Mosko Handler, Early Life and Family.
jwa.org/encyclopedia/article/handler-ruth-mosko

kansaspublicradio.org, Olive Ann Beech: the Woman from Waverly Who Changed Aviation History.
kansaspublicradio.org/commentaries-news/2019-06-12/olive-ann-beech-the-woman-from-waverly-who-changed-aviation-history

kent.edu, Designer Archives - Pauline Trigère.
kent.edu/museum/designer-archives

latimes.com, Pauline Trigere, 93; Fashion Designer Bridged Cultures.
latimes.com/archives/la-xpm-2002-feb-15-me-trigere15-story.html

legacy.com, Bette Nesmith Graham: Innovator.
legacy.com/news/bette-nesmith-graham-innovator/

lemelson.mit.edu, Bette Graham Liquid Paper.
lemelson.mit.edu/resources/bette-graham

linkedin.com, Coco Chanel legacy as designer, Daniella Urgelles.
linkedin.com/pulse/coco-chanel-legacy-designer-daniela-urgelles

linkedin.com, Stephen Chen, President at Joyce Chen Foods.
linkedin.com/in/stephen-chen-906b1531

livinginfiftiesfashion.com, The Many Talents of Pauline Trigère.
livinginfiftiesfashion.com/2017/11/the-many-talents-of-pauline-trigere.html

Lydia E. Pinkham | American businesswoman | Britannica.
britannica.com/biography/Lydia-E-Pinkham

Lydia E. Pinkham Memorial Clinic (1922).
mass.historicbuildingsct.com/?p=724

Lydia Pinkham | History of American Women.
womenhistoryblog.com/2012/07/lydia-pinkham.html

Lydia Pinkham Was an Inventor and Marketer - ThoughtCo.
thoughtco.com/lydia-pinkham-biography-3529532

Lydia Pinkham® Herbal Compound - Numark Brands.
numarkbrands.com/products/lydia-pinkham-herbal-compound

Madam C. J. Walker.
history.com/topics/black-history/madame-c-j-walker

Madam C. J. Walker | Academic Influence - What is C.J. Walker's legacy?
academicinfluence.com/people/madam-cj-walker

Madam C. J. Walker | Biography, Company, & Facts.
britannica.com/biography/Madam-C-J-Walker

Madam C. J. Walker | National Postal Museum.
postalmuseum.si.edu/exhibition/women-on-stamps-part-2-professionals-and-philanthropists-enhancing-lives/madam-cj-walker

messynesstchic.com, Adored by Many, but Loved by Chanel: A Forgotten Parisian It Girl.
messynessychic.com/2019/07/19/adored-by-many-but-loved-by-chanel-a-forgotten-parisian-it-girl/

National Beauty Culturists and Benevolent Association.
images.indianahistory.org/digital/collection/m0399/id/11121

nationalhumanitiescenter.org - Eliza Lucas Pinckney, Letters & Memoranda, 1740-1762.
nationalhumanitiescenter.org/pds/becomingamer/peoples/text5/elizapinckney.pdf

nearlymeonline.com, Nearly Me.

news24.com, Chanel's complex legacy.
news24.com/w24/style/fashion/style/chanels-complex-legacy-20211224

nps.gov, Eliza Lucas Pinckney - National Park Service.
nps.gov/chpi/learn/historyculture/eliza-lucas-pinckney.htm

nytimes.com, A Million-Dollar Business from a Mastectomy.
nytimes.com/1977/06/19/archives/a-milliondollar-business-from-a-mastectomy.html

nytimes.com, Anita Roddick, Body Shop Founder, Dies at 64.
nytimes.com/2007/09/12/world/europe/12roddick.html

nytimes.com, Fashion Designer Hires Negro Model; Beverly Valdes Said to Be First of Race to Work on 7th Ave. Magazines, Ad Agency Officials Hesitant to Employ Negroes.
nytimes.com/1961/06/23/archives/fashion-designer-hires-negro-model-beverly-valdes-said-to-be-first.html

nytimes.com, Overlooked No More: Bette Nesmith Graham, Who Invented Liquid Paper.
nytimes.com/2018/07/11/obituaries/bette-nesmith-graham-overlooked.html

Parminder Vir OBE (LinkedIn) - Frequently Asked Questions (FAQs) On Starting A Business - Part 1.
linkedin.com/pulse/frequently-asked-questions-faqs-starting-business-part-vir-obe

pbs.org, Ruth Handler, Barbie.
pbs.org/wgbh/theymadeamerica/whomade/handler_hi.html

pressreader.com, The Best of the Best.
pressreader.com/south-africa/african-pilot/20210701/281655373051562

prezi.com, Anita Roddick.
prezi.com/d7y5htp6mhce/anita-roddick/

refashioninghistory.com, Pauline Trigère.
refashioninghistory.com/2017/05/23/pauline- trigere/

referenceforbusiness.com, Beech Aircraft Corporation.
referenceforbusiness.com/history2/17/Beech-Aircraft-Corporation. html

rpx2.com, Women in Leadership: Anita Roddick.
rpx2.com/women-leadership-anita-roddick/

sandiegoairandspace.org, Olive Beech.
sandiegoairandspace.org/hall-of-fame/honoree/olive-beech

sps-aviation.com, Olive Ann Beech (1903-1993).
sps-aviation.com/story/?id=2392&h=Olive-Ann-Beech-1903-1993

statista.com, Global brand value of Chanel from 2017 to 2022. statista.com/statistics/1010860/chanel-brand-value-worldwide/

Sundial Brands Unveils Madam by Madam C.J. Walker. beautypackaging.com/contents/view_breaking-news/2022-02-01/sundial-brands-unveils-madam-by-madam-cj-walker

teenvogue.com, Study Shows Barbie Dolls Negatively Impact Young Girls' Body Image.
teenvogue.com/story/barbie-body-image-study

The philanthropy of Madam C.J. Walker, 1867-1919.
core.ac.uk/download/pdf/46959277.pdf

The Scaffold - Lily the Pink - YouTube, WiggyVideos.
youtube.com/watch?v=2x8D4T--0v4

thebodyshop.com, Our Values.
thebodyshop.com/en-gb/about-us/brand-values/a/a00006

theconversation.com, The real story of the Barbie doll: strong female leadership behind the scenes.
theconversation.com/the-real-story-of-the-barbie-doll-strong-female-leadership-behind-the-scenes-118708

theguardian.com, Dame Anita Roddick | Business.
theguardian.com/news/2007/sep/12/guardianobituaries. business

theguardian.com, L'Oréal buys Body Shop for £652m - The Guardian.
theguardian.com/business/2006/mar/17/retail.money

theroddickfoundation.org

thestar.com.my, Chanel's new identity: sporty style.
thestar.com.my/lifestyle/women/fashion/2014/09/10/chanels-new-identity-sporty-style

thisdayinaviation.com/3-september-1936

thisiscapitalism.com, Beyond Barbie: The Legacy of Mattel Founder Ruth Handler.
thisiscapitalism.com/beyond-barbie-the-legacy-of-mattel-founder-ruth-handler/

thisismoney.co.uk, How a £4,000 Body Shop loan made £146m. thisismoney.co.uk/money/news/article-1696860/How-a-4000-Body-Shop-loan-made-146m.html

thoughtco.com, Biography of Bette Nesmith Graham, Inventor of Liquid Paper - Early life.
thoughtco.com/ liquid-paper-bette-nesmith-graham-1992092

threadsmagazine.com, Pauline Trigère - Profiles in Sewing History - A lauded and sought-after designer.
threadsmagazine.com/2021/09/21/pauline-trigere-profiles-in-sewing-history

time.com, How Poverty Shaped Coco Chanel.
time.com/ 3994196/coco-chanel-1883/

tompsc.com, Charles Pinckney.
tompsc.com/289/Charles-Pinckney

Tori Barnes-Brus, Chapter 4. Savior of her Sex, Lydia e. Pinkham.
kuscholarworks.ku.edu/bitstream/handle/1808/7881/BarnesBrus_ku_0099D_11303_DATA_1.pdf

us.trigere.com, Heritage - 1972 - 1976 Vive la France!
us.trigere.com/pages/heritage

Was Lydia E. Pinkham the Queen of Quackery? - JSTOR Daily.
daily.jstor.org/was-lydia-e-pinkham-the-queen-of-quackery/

washingtonpost.com, Award-Winning Designer Pauline Trigere, 93, Dies.
washingtonpost.com/archive/local/2002/02/15/award-winning-designer-pauline-trigere-93-dies/5e452645-d7f8-4e60-bb08-1474b26eb5f3/

What are the biggest challenges to starting a business?
forbes.com/sites/abdoriani/2021/11/18/the-biggest-challenges-faced-by-startups/?sh=564006624956

Who Was Madam C.J. Walker's Third Husband, Charles.
oprahdaily.com/entertainment/tv-movies/a31941155/madam-cj-walker-husband-charles-joseph

wikipedia.org, Ruth Handler.
en.wikipedia.org/wiki/Ruth_Handler

wikipedia.org, Bette Nesmith Graham.
en.wikipedia.org/wiki/Bette_Nesmith_Graham

wikipedia.org, Coco Chanel.
en.wikipedia.org/wiki/ Coco_Chanel

wikipedia.org, Eliza Lucas.
en.wikipedia.org/wiki/ Eliza_Lucas

wikipedia.org, Gabrielle Dorziat.
en.wikipedia.org/wiki/ Gabrielle_Dorziat

wikipedia.org, John Locke.
en.wikipedia.org/wiki/John_Locke

wikipedia.org, Joyce Chen (chef).
en.wikipedia.org/wiki/Joyce_Chen_(chef)

wikipedia.org, Liquid paper.
en.wikipedia.org/wiki/Liquid_Paper

wikipedia.org, Lydia Pinkham.
en.wikipedia.org/wiki/Lydia_Pinkham

wikipedia.org, Madam C. J. Walker Manufacturing Company.
en.wikipedia.org/wiki/Madam_C._J._Walker_Manufacturing_Company

wikipedia.org, Madam C.J. Walker.
en.wikipedia.org/wiki/Madam_C._J._Walker

wikipedia.org, Olive Ann Beech.
en.wikipedia.org/wiki/Olive_Ann_Beech

wikipedia.org, Pauline Trigère.
en.wikipedia.org/wiki/Pauline_Trig%C3%A8re

wikipedia.org, The Allure of Chanel.
en.wikipedia.org/wiki/The_Allure_of_Chanel

wikipedia.org, WERD (historic radio station).
en.wikipedia.org/wiki/WERD_(historic_radio_station)

wikipedia.org, Wright Brothers Memorial Trophy.
en.wikipedia.org/wiki/Wright_Brothers_Memorial_Trophy

Williams, Harriet Simons. "Eliza Lucas and Her Family: Before the Letterbook". South Carolina Historical Magazine. 99 (3): 259-279.

vintagepatterns.fandom.com, McCall's 1048, Pauline Trigère.
vintagepatterns.fandom.com/wiki/McCall%27s_1048

womenhistoryblog.com, Eliza Lucas Pinckney.
womenhistoryblog.com/2008/09/eliza-lucas-pinckney.html

womenshistory.org, Joyce Chen.
womenshistory.org/education-resources/biographies/joyce-chen

YouTube - Madam C.J. Walker's TWO DOLLARS AND A DREAM | Trailer.
youtube.com/watch?v=mXdqWW8Tkfk

1. Williams, Harriet Simons. "Eliza Lucas and Her Family: Before the Letterbook". South Carolina Historical Magazine. 99 (3): 259–279.
2. Elise Pinckney and Marvin R. Zahniser, eds., The Letterbook of Eliza Lucas Pinckney: Intriguing Letters by One of Colonial America's Most Accomplished Women, Eliza Lucas Pinckney.
3. Campbell, P. S. (1922). "Nostrum and Quack Evil". The Public Health Journal.
4. Was Lydia E. Pinkham the Queen of Quackery? - JSTOR Daily
5. Tori Barnes-Brus, Chapter 4. Saviour of her Sex, Lydia e. Pinkham
6. Bundles, A'Lelia (2001). On Her Own Ground: The Life and Times of Madam C. J. Walker.
7. Biography of Madam C.J. Walker, American Entrepreneur
8. Ibid.
9. Charles-Roux, Edmonde (1981). Chanel and Her World. London: Weidenfeld and Nicolson.
10. messynesstchic.com, Adored by Many, but Loved by Chanel: A Forgotten Parisian It Girl
11. express.co.uk, Coco Chanel's decade long affair with Duke of Westminster ended with proposal
12. thestar.com.my, Chanel's new identity: sporty style
13. wikipedia.org, The Allure of Chanel.
14. linkedin.com, Coco Chanel legacy as designer, Daniella Urgelles.
15. livinginfiftiesfashion.com, The Many Talents of Pauline Trigère.
16. theconversation.com, The real story of the Barbie doll: strong female leadership behind the scenes.
17. jwa.org, Ruth Mosko Handler, Illness and Legacy.
18. joycechenfoods.com, Savouring the Legacy of Joyce Chen – Her Story.
19. cnbc.com, How inventing Liquid Paper got a secretary fired and then turned her into an exec worth $25 million.
20. prezi.com, Anita Roddick.
21. theguardian.com, Anita Roddick dies aged 64 | Business | The Guardian.
22. rpx2.com, Women in Leadership: Anita Roddick.
23. Ibid.

24. theguardian.com, Anita Roddick dies aged 64 | Business | The Guardian.

Printed in Great Britain
by Amazon

55588966R00069